Sunny Side Up

Sunny Side Up

by

ALMA BARKMAN

MOODY PRESS

CHICAGO

© 1977 by
THE MOODY BIBLE INSTITUTE
OF CHICAGO

Library of Congress Cataloging in Publication Data

Barkman, Alma.
  Sunny-side up.

  1. Women—Prayer—books and devotions—English.
I. Title.

BV4844.B34   242'.6'33   77-7048

ISBN 0-8024-8431-X

10 11 12 Printing/LC/Year 89

Printed in the United States of America

Dedicated to my husband,
Leo,
who in a sudden
burst of inspiration suggested
the title *Sunny Side Up*

INTRODUCTION

You've probably heard it said of an optimistic person, "She's a good egg!"

It's a nice compliment, as opposed to the contrary.

But how do these "good eggs" meet their day? Scrambled? Hard-boiled? I doubt it! They are among the cheery souls who roll out of bed and greet each new morning "sunny side up."

Not all of us can claim such envious distinction, but the Christian homemaker has a better reason than most to maintain a cheerful disposition. It is hoped that the articles shared in this book will be an added encouragement to her as she seeks a touch of humor and spiritual meaning in each little episode of life.

1. MINUS THE HALO

And I will bring a piece of bread, that you may refresh yourselves (Genesis 18:5a).

We have always used an old-fashioned toaster with collapsible sides. I dare say it burns the toast as adequately as any pop-up model with a faulty thermostat. Still, people act surprised when they see it adorning my kitchen table.

I hasten to explain that in this household we eat homemade bread—twenty-four hours a day, or so it seems. Anyway, you can't sliver puny slices from a loaf of homemade bread. Only the stuff from the bakery comes preshaven; the slices are so thin that if you leave them a second too long in the toaster you have two sheets of carbon paper.

That is the main reason I refuse to be swayed by all the propaganda about updating my appliances. If I buy a pop-up toaster, I have to buy the bread to fit it.

Such subtle pressures also exist in religious circles. Not content with the choice morsels found in the Word of God, we have people today who rely upon experiences as their spiritual staff of life. Claiming to be "on fire for the Lord," they urge others to follow their example, when in reality much of their talk reveals a very immature, undernourished faith.

Instead of becoming carbon-copy Christians, striving to imitate the experiences of others, we are to discern God's will in a personal way by applying the bread of life to a realistic life-style.

For the Christian homemaker this may mean summoning up all the resources at her disposal. Regularly nourished by the Word of God, however, she will be able to meet her responsibilities with optimism and understanding. Real blessing and contentment are in store for the woman who looks upon her role as a unique, God-given challenge, "for by this some have entertained angels without knowing it" (Hebrews 13:2*a*).

The "angels" you entertain may have tousled hair and jam on their faces, but the rewards are just as great.

2. OF MORE VALUE THAN SPARROWS

Are not two sparrows sold for a cent? And yet not one of them will fall to the ground apart from your Father (Matthew 10:29).

Last Saturday morning our neighbor girl emerged from her room in a state of shock. She had discovered, upon waking, that her faithful budgie bird had gone to his reward.

Now, you don't bury your one and only budgie in his birthday feathers. You hunt high and low for a suitable box and fix him up properly. Then while Dad and your dog look on, you pay your last respects.

Appropriately enough, when the mourners returned from the interment ceremony out behind the raspberry patch, Tennessee Ernie Ford was singing "His Eye Is on the Sparrow."

The reaction was not what one might expect.

"So what if God cares about dumb old sparrows?" Cindy cried indignantly. "Blueboy wasn't just a sparrow. He was a *budgie* bird!"

I sympathize. We all have our days when we feel God has overlooked our problems in favor of someone much less worthy of His attention. The job promotion goes to someone else you think is less capable; the people with a lower income manage to buy the nice new house; you don't receive the recognition you feel you deserve; you're cheated out of that new dress because the car needs repairs; other families go on vacations that yours can never even dream about—the list is endless.

We need to remember that God's love encompasses all

His children, not just a select few. It is not His neglect which fills us with self-pity. It is our own feelings of pride and jealousy. We want God to favor us and show us some special attention, not because He loves us, but because we feel we deserve it. We demand our own way like spoiled children, when all along the heavenly Father knows exactly what is best for us.

If we set aside all feelings of envy and examine our lives carefully, we will see that whatever God has given or withheld was for our own benefit. An attitude of acceptance toward His will softens the blows and helps us to adjust. "Why are you in despair, O my soul? And why are you disturbed within me? Hope in God, for I shall again praise Him, the help of my countenance, and my God" (Psalm 43:5).

3. HOME FREE

For what I fear comes upon me, and what I dread befalls me (Job 3:25).

I have just returned from escorting our youngest son to school. First-time mothers were milling around the principal's office, dabbing their moist eyes and crying on each other's shoulders. I know how they feel.

The day you enroll your firstborn, it's a whole new "bawl" game. You suddenly see your impetuous, stubborn independent son as a timid, clinging, frightened, little five-year-old, thrust out into the big, bad world before his time. You try to restrain yourself, but the urge to snatch him away from the clutches of the principal and restore him to the family nest is a very strong maternal instinct.

The fourth child around, it's a different story. You see the twinkle in Junior's eyes as he anticipates this new adventure. You admire his ability to fend for himself, and somehow you *know* that school will be just the thing for him. Besides, aren't you looking forward to a rest yourself?

Unlike some mothers, I have tasted freedom once before. I know what it's like to finish the laundry without umpteen trips upstairs to look in on Junior. I know what it's like to sew a dress or bake a cake without ten busy little fingers around to help. In short, you get a lot more done with a lot less effort. When the oldest two boys were both in school, we even had time to build a house.

The stork must have found the new chimney attractive. The two youngest children arrived in rapid succession, putting an end to all established routine. Now after six years,

12

I am looking forward to my second stint of undisturbed housekeeping. From now on, I will have the privilege of choosing my day's itinerary.

Some women tell me that just the prospect of such freedom is frightening. Caught up in the endless merry-go-round of attending to preschoolers, they have allowed family demands to dictate their routine. Now that the children are in school, these women have little or no initiative to undertake projects on their own. As a result, many of them seek jobs outside the home, not as a supplement to family income, but as a source of personal fulfillment.

It seems unfortunate that so many of the skills and crafts that were once a source of pride and enjoyment are being sacrificed for a nine-to-five job. True, gifts and talents differ with the individual, but I wonder if some of us are simply choosing the easy way out instead of exercising our will power to make profitable use of leisure time. We should take time to discipline ourselves in more worthwhile pursuits, enriching those around us by deepening our own quality of life.

"Instruct those who are rich in this present world not to be conceited or to fix their hope on the uncertainty of riches, but on God, who richly supplies us with all things to enjoy. Instruct them to do good, to be rich in good works, to be generous and ready to share, storing up for themselves the treasure of a good foundation for the future, so that they may take hold of that which is life indeed" (1 Timothy 6: 17-19).

4. THE LITTLE MATTERS

*For on the way they had discussed with one another
which of them was the greatest. And sitting down,
He called the twelve and said to them, "If any one wants
to be first, he shall be last of all, and servant of all"*
(Mark 9:34-35).

Very early in the morning, the back entrance to our house
begins filling up with an assortment of children. About half
of them belong to us. The rest have discovered a very simple password: "Is Susie (or Tommy or Jerry) ready for
school yet?"

I cannot possibly offend them, all innocence and overshoes shivering on my doorstep, so one by one, I invite them
in.

"Doesn't your mother even go to work?" The question
is directed at our girl, who still has her mouth filled with
cornflakes. She shakes her head in the negative.

Next question: "Then what does she *do* all day?"

The snow from their overshoes is melting into great, dirty
puddles on the floor. I know *one* thing I will have to do
today.

"We're wearing our new outfits. Our mommy bought
them for us if we'd be good." Those unfinished efforts lit-
tering my sewing room flit across my mind, but there is little
time for guilt complexes. I go down the hall to direct op-
erations in the bathroom. "Susie, comb your hair! Tommy,
your face is still dirty."

I come back and start sorting out overshoes and mittens,
only to discover a few extra pairs. The visitors, you see,

14

have taken off their snowsuits in order to show me their new outfits. Now there are twice as many kids to dress.

"Hey, those are my mitts!"

"She's got her boots on the wrong feet!"

"Don't let the cat out!"

"I can't find my book!"

And then, "Mrs. Barkman, please, I have to go to the bathroom."

Now I know why it says the first shall be last. It is the natural consequence of not keeping our priorities straight.

To strive for recognition, to "elbow our way" to the top, to demand attention from others, indicates a desire to be first, a thirst for power. How humiliating to face defeat due to some "inconsequential" oversight which undermines the impression we wish to make. The unpaid bill, the hasty word, the "forgotten friend" may one day destroy our reputation as a conscientious, considerate person.

We must never consider any facet of our lives as unimportant. Scrubbing floors, changing diapers, or running errands may not seem very edifying to the Lord at the moment, but remember God's commendation, "Well done, good and faithful slave; you were faithful with a few things, I will put you in charge of many things, enter into the joy of your master" (Matthew 25:21).

5. ENCOURAGING SPADEWORK

The memory of the righteous is blessed (Proverbs 10: 7a).

I miss her this time of year. When we moved into this neighborhood, she lived in Oak Grove Cottage. It was a do-it-yourself home she had pieced together with her own hands, a fragile structure in comparison to the rugged oaks which dwarfed it. Shasta daisies grew wild and rebellious along her front fence, in sharp contrast to the struggling clumps of maroon dahlias just behind them.

Green-thumb enthusiasts half her age could not have kept pace with her as she dug, weeded, raked, and hoed. Nor were her interests restricted to her own yard.

"My! Just look at that garden of yours! Why, I remember when nothing but ragweeds grew back there. Now just look at that corn!" Ashamed of our own impatience, we would dig in a little deeper.

She was convinced that homegrown vegetables and preserves were the secret of robust good health. Discovering a few jars of pickles or fruit cooling on my counter, she would exclaim with delight, "My, but that's prettier than any picture! And look at the rosy cheeks on those babies!"

She is gone now.

A few defiant daisies still bloom along her lot line, the only evidence of her handiwork to escape the bulldozer blade. Oak Grove Cottage is no more.

I miss her this time of year. The jars of tomatoes and peaches are cooling on my counter, reflecting red and gold sunbeams across the kitchen. The back step is laden with baskets full of cucumbers, dill, carrots, beans, and tomatoes. Our six-year-old son is toting in armloads of corn on the cob, his face flushed with pride and anticipation. Such rich dividends from our garden seem a fitting memorial to a friend whose words were a constant source of encouragement.

I realize anew how important it is for us to uphold one another in all areas of life. A word of commendation here or a bit of helpful advice there can make a distinct difference for someone who is struggling along with feelings of loneliness or inadequacy.

The interest you take at some point along the way may prove to be an enriching factor in the lives of others for years to come, and "you will be like a watered garden, and like a spring of water whose waters do not fail" (Isaiah 58: 11*b*).

6. GODLY PATIENCE

The Lord is not slow about His promise, as some count slowness, but is patient toward you, not wishing for any to perish but for all to come to repentance (2 Peter 3:9).

Old Gramps is a patient man. He just never gets tired of waiting. He and Grandma have been married fifty years, and I dare say he has spent most of that time just waiting for her.

He waited for her at the altar of the rickety old country church when her wedding dress snagged on the splinters in the floorboards.

He waited for her at the bedside when the stork got hung up delivering the young 'uns.

He waited for her with the horse and buggy while she swapped butter and eggs at the country store.

He waited for her at the parking meter while she shopped in the city and got stuck with her parcels in one of those newfangled revolving doors.

Everywhere they went, he waited for her.

He was her companion when lonely, her comfort when grief-stricken, her support when shaky.

He advised her when she needed it and even when she didn't.

Then at their golden anniversary, Gramps got to his feet, his spindly old legs shaking, and with trembling voice said, "I'd like to pay tribute to my bride of fifty years. I could never have achieved a thing without her."

Is that how God looks upon my relationship to Him? As

a member of that body of believers referred to in the Scriptures as "the Bride of Christ," I realize how often I have kept Him waiting. There were the years when I debated whether to commit my life to Him. Afterward there were times when He waited for me to lead someone else into the circle of His love.

There were times when He waited for me to "feed the newborn babes," to teach Sunday school or read a story to our own children or perhaps lead a Bible study.

There were times He waited while I sorted out my stewardship and decided which dollars should be invested in His service.

And there were times when my priorities got snagged in the revolving social scene and I carefully reconsidered my purpose in life.

And all the while, the Lord waits patiently, standing by to encourage and comfort each one of us in our Christian responsibilities. Despite our failures and our weaknesses, He still considers us a vital part of His intended purpose: "Therefore, we are ambassadors for Christ, as though God were entreating through us; we beg you on behalf of Christ, be reconciled to God" (2 Corinthians 5:20).

7. "FAITHING" THE FUTURE

*For now we see in a mirror dimly, but then face to face;
now I know in part, but then I shall know fully just as
I also have been fully known* (1 Corinthians 13:12).

Those windows they put in oven doors have taken the fun
and suspense out of bake day. Remember when Grandma
used to stoke up the fire and prepare to bake gingerbread?
The smell of woodsmoke and molasses still mingle in my
memory. With cheeks pink from the heat and eyes shining
with anticipation, we hovered about the stove, waiting for
that magic moment. By some intuitive feeling Grandma
knew exactly when to open the door. *Voilà!* A gingerbread
magnificent!

With all our modern switches and gadgets and timers,
however, I doubt if we can boast a higher success rate than
Grandma. When things went wrong, she could at least
blame it on the stove.

Today we have no such excuse. You put the cake in the
oven and stand there, wringing your hands while you watch
it flop. The sense of failure you experience is entirely your
own, the pain that much greater because the anguish is pro-
longed. Grandma at least remained optimistic until the moment of truth.

I have heard people say that the future should be revealed
to us so we could prepare ourselves for the inevitable. I can
tell you right here and now that my outlook on bake day
was far healthier before we bought a stove with a window
in the oven. About all I do now is stand in front of the oven
window, fretting over my imminent failures.

If life were like that, the drama would be gone before the curtain lifted, the outcome known long before the challenge arose, the mystery solved before the book ended.

God knows what He is about. A few peeks here and there, perhaps, but the rest of the time the just shall live by faith. "And without faith it is impossible to please Him, for he who comes to God must believe that He is, and that He is a rewarder of those who seek Him" (Hebrews 11:6).

8. DRIVEN TO AND FRO?

God is our refuge and strength, a very present help in trouble (Psalm 46:1).

Last Sunday the menfolk informed me that, due to un-expected circumstances, I would have to drive the truck home from church.

Now, if the vehicle in question had been one of those slick half-ton trucks with chrome trim which affluent farmers use as status symbols, I would not have objected.

The truck in this family, however, bears close resemblance to the celebrated jumping frog. Green with brown rust spots, it is weighted down at the back by a load of broken con-crete.

Even at that, it does not exactly hug the road, because there is a quarter-turn play in the steering wheel. Every time we approached a corner, I had to resort to the old hand-over-hand bus-driver technique, whereupon the little kids burst forth with an updated version of the "Old Gray Mare":

> Old bus driver sat on a 'lectric chair,
> Burned off his underwear,
> Chased by a grizzly bear,
> Old bus driver, speed up a little bit,
> Many more miles to home.

All in all, it was a very humiliating experience for a lady still decked up in her church finery. The Sunday drivers were very gracious, however, even when I fumbled around for the gearshift in the middle of intersections.

As we rumbled up the driveway, I kept thinking of Alexander the Great. "There are," he said, "no more worlds to conquer."

Now that depends on where we look for our challenges! Often I tend to "steer clear" of the very areas in which I am most needed, simply because I lack confidence in myself.

Occasionally, however, I find I am placed in unusual circumstances where I really have no alternative. I must assume responsibility despite lack of training or preparation, despite the fear of failure. At such times I learn anew to commit *everything* to the Lord and rely on His providential hand.

We can be assured that where it is folly to stand still, God literally coaxes us to move along through an inner strength He Himself provides.

Sensing His will, but conceding our initial lack of trust, we look back upon such anxious moments and exclaim, "I can do all things through Him who strengthens me" (Philippians 4:13).

9. SELFISH OR SATISFIED?

I tell you, even though he will not get up and give him anything because he is his friend, yet because of his persistence he will get up and give him as much as he needs (Luke 11:8).

I think the tomcat has a crush on the refrigerator. He sits for hours mooning over its contents, a faraway look in his great, green eyes. Every so often when temptation gets the better of him, he tries to charm the door open by purring sweet nothings into my ear.

If there's no response, he curls up in a fresh patch of warm sunlight and continues staring at the refrigerator with wistful gaze.

There's no way I can open that refrigerator door without his knowing it. Even if he's sleeping in the far corner of the basement, he comes galloping up the stairs at top speed the minute the door is opened.

As I stand there debating what I need, he bulldozes between my feet and tries to tell me what to make for supper. Tomcats can be very vocal. I hook him around the midriff with my toe and shut the door. He is developing a permament kink in his caudal appendage from getting it pinched so often, but he never gives up.

As I move toward the stove, he winds in and out between my feet until progress is all but impossible. I am convinced that every tomcat's dream is to trip the cook and capture a windfall of sausages. In desperation I toss him a delectable morsel or two.

When it comes to getting what we want out of life, we,

like the tomcat, can become a persistent nuisance. Some people display a constant attitude of self-pity, hoping society will show sympathy for their need. If that fails, they adopt the opposite extreme, ever alert to opportunities which may work to their advantage. Instead of waiting their turn, they forge ahead without considering the rights of others, whether it be in the matter of job promotion or just personal recognition.

Intent on achieving immediate satisfaction, we may sacrifice friendship and genuine fulfillment in the pursuit of our own selfish goals. The subtle hints, the constant reminders, and the overbearing attitude may be ways in which the world tries to get ahead, but they are not becoming to one who claims to be a follower of Christ. "But godliness actually is a means of great gain, when accompanied by contentment" (1 Timothy 6:6).

10. REVEALING EVIDENCE

If therefore you are presenting your offering at the altar, and there remember that your brother has something against you, leave your offering there before the altar, and go your way; first be reconciled to your brother, and then come and present your offering (Matthew 5:23-24).

The doctor pauses midway through the examination.

"Hm" is all he says.

"Hm" means I am to have an X ray. He scribbles his suspicions on a little slip of paper. "Take this down to the lab," he orders.

Now, X-ray labs are very impersonal places. I not only dispense with my name; I am told to shed my clothes as well. "Put this on and wait your turn." The girl hands me a paper gown. "You may leave your boots on." (In case of fire, maybe?)

I am led to my stall. About two feet square, it is furnished with a stool, a clothes hook, and the covers from two magazines. It's rather difficult, but I manage to get into my paper gown. Every time I bend over, my posterior bumps the wall. Bump. Bump. The herd is restless tonight.

I hear them call my stall number. It is tempting to answer with a low "moo," but I restrain myself. I would hate to cause a stampede.

I hobble along the chute in my paper gown and rustle up onto the table. "Boots and all," says the technician, as if they will prevent me from dying from exposure. The machine whirs and clicks a couple of times, and I'm told to go back to my stall and await the results.

X rays are not at all becoming. "You mean to tell me I look like *that* inside?"

"Sure," says the technician. "Everybody does."

I begin to wonder what a spiritual X ray would reveal. Are there fractured relationships that need to be mended? Are there priorities that have slipped out of place? What about the splintered allegiance I offer with the futile hope of satisfying both God and man?

Sometimes God sets us aside by circumstances in order that we may examine our walk and repair the broken places in our relationship with Him. However hesitant we may be about approaching a brother whom we have offended, it is up to us to take the initiative. Broken bones, though painful, mend correctly when they are set and held securely in place by a cast. Severed relationships heal only in an atmosphere of godly love and forgiveness. "There is no fear in love; for perfect love casts out fear" (1 John 4:18*a*).

11. SOMEONE MISSES YOU

I lie awake. I have become like a lonely bird on a house-top (Psalm 102:7).

I hear the city siren blow the 11:00 PM curfew. Locating some loose change in my purse, I sneak down to the empty hotel hobby. The dime jangles into the pay telephone and hits rock bottom. Dialing the familiar number, I wait for him to answer.

One ring—another. He answers the third with a gruff "Hello?"

The operator interrupts. "That will be nintey-five cents for the first three minutes, madam." I deposit the required amount.

"Hi!" I say. "Are you getting along OK? How are the kids? Do they miss me? Has there been any mail?" My cheerful tone belies the anguish.

"Everything's fine!" he assures me. "The kids are in bed, and I've finally finished the dishes. It's only nine o'clock here, you know."

"Yes, I know. I just thought I would call to see how you were."

"We're fine! Really we are."

I was afraid of that.

Loneliness is often compounded by the feeling that others don't need us. We want to be appreciated in our home, our work, or our church. The fact that these places can carry on without our contribution is a rather painful experience.

What we tend to overlook is the *quality* we lend by our presence. The home without a mother can still function, but

28

in a superficial way. If you are not there to care about the hurts and scratches, to lend a listening ear, or to prepare a snack after school, your children are missing a certain quality of life that can never be recaptured.

If there is one less teacher on the Sunday school staff or one less lady in the mission circle or one less in the choir loft, it is not just a mere vacancy. It is a certain quality missing from that church, a quality that can only be represented by your presence.

There are times when we are set aside by circumstances beyond our control, but we should never allow loneliness to destroy our sense of worth. God has created us for individual purposes, and life is made richer for someone because of *you.*

12. BURNING OIL?

My sons, do not be negligent now, for the Lord has chosen you to stand before Him, to minister to Him (2 Chronicles 29:11*a*).

Ever since the teenager acquired a car, mealtime has been little more than a pit stop. What was once stimulating conversation now goes something like this:

"How come my cornflakes are soggy again?"

"Maybe they got tired waiting while you changed spark plugs."

"Aw, c'mon, Mom. Just cuz you don't know a thing about cars doesn't mean Dad and I can't talk about 'em."

"OK. But don't blame me for the rubber eggs."

"Yeah, you're right. I could use them for motor mounts. And this cold toast! It's so limp I could wring it out and use it for a grease rag."

At noon he comes home stoked with fresh enthusiasm. It seems the shop teacher is giving a course in motor mechanics. As a result, we don't eat lunch; we just pause for a tune-up.

At suppertime we are treated to a wheel alignment, a lube job, new points—the whole bit.

"If I were you I would just add a quart of oil."

"Whaddya mean? I'm not low on oil!" He stomps out indignantly and disappears in a cloud of blue smoke.

We can become so preoccupied with new and exciting challenges that we overlook the necessity of regular maintenance. No matter how smoothly things are running at present, my Christian walk will gradually grind to a halt unless sustained through Bible study and prayer. The purpose of a complete "overhaul" through faith in Christ is soon defeated if I abuse God's grace through neglect. "Burning oil" I call it, ignoring the promptings of the Spirit and squandering my time and efforts elsewhere.

Other people can usually detect this inconsistency simply by observing my life. Like the teenager, however, I often resent their good advice, quite confident that my own wisdom will carry me through.

Just as repair work and maintenance can never be separated, grace and obedience must go hand in hand or else I become spiritually immobile, unable to move in the direction God would have me go. "Behold, to obey is better than sacrifice" (1 Samuel 15:22b).

13. CAKE-TRAY CONFUSION

And why do you look at the speck in your brother's eye, but do not notice the log that is in your own eye? (Matthew 7:3).

Years ago friend hubby gave me a fancy cake tray. I was so proud of it that I made the mistake of displaying it on top of the refrigerator. I haven't found it since.

No doubt it's there somewhere, covered by a confusion difficult to describe. From my present vantage point I can see one hammer, three screwdrivers, a pocket computer, a transistor radio, and some obsolete mail.

Up closer, I notice two sticks of gum, a razor blade, one apple core, two check stubs, and seven and a half pencils. Aside from that, there are three saucedishes full of nuts, bolts, and nails, plus the bottom half of a bleach jug bulging with enough machinery to build a stock car.

I wish some genius would design a refrigerator with a dome roof so that nothing would adhere to it.

Unfortunately, I would be caught at my own tricks. In addition to all that hardware mentioned previously, I deliberately overlooked three spools of thread, a pair of scissors, one potholder, and a wilted geranium. Oh, yes! And my cake tray.

How often we thoughtlessly lead the way in matters which later go beyond our control! Little did I realize that I was setting a trend when I placed that cake tray on top of the refrigerator. Following my example, the rest of the family soon added their contributions, simply because it was a convenient place to put things. Looking at that accumulation of junk, it was easy to accuse others but difficult to concede that I had probably led the way.

Once a bad habit is instilled, we all know how hard it is to break it. Before condemning others, we must examine our own lives to be sure we are not guilty of setting a poor example. "Let no one look down on your youthfulness, but rather in speech, conduct, love, faith and purity, show yourself an example of those who believe" (1 Timothy 4:12).

14. A DEAD GIVEAWAY

Does not the ear test words, as the palate tastes its food?
(Job 12:11).

For years now the supermarkets have been selling chicken pulp disguised as poultry. Dressed up in all sorts of fancy names—fryers, broilers, roasters—they thought they had the public fooled into believing that their chickens were the real thing.

Not me. I can taste the difference anytime between a genuine homegrown product and one of those assembly-line models. Last spring I even went into partnership with a friend, and we bought a hundred chickens. Cockerels, to be exact. Actually, we had to take the hatchery's word for it.

On July 1 we went out to the farm to make their acquaintance.

"Tell me," asked my friend, "do those look like roosters to you?"

"Well, don't they crow?"

"I don't believe they've even tried."

It was time we looked into this matter so we walked over closer to examine the flock. "Now look at that one over there. Doesn't that look like a hen to you?"

"And it even walks like one!"

"You're right!" she exclaimed. "A hen sort of waddles, and a rooster struts."

The next ten minutes were spent leaning over the fence debating the issue. When we informed the menfolk of our suspicions, they were highly amused.

"Laugh if you like," we told them, "but women always walk differently than men."

"Oh, we don't deny that, but these are chickens."

"So maybe a woman walks like an old hen."

"You said it. We didn't."

At that point we decided it was in our best interests to let the case rest.

A few weeks later I received a letter from my friend. "Guess what!" she wrote. "They're crowing!"

And with that choice bit of evidence, we were able to declare the file officially closed. The menfolk were subsequently dismissed as witnesses, the hatchery acquitted of fraud, and the roosters remanded on a charge of false pretenses.

I wonder how often I, as a Christian, confuse people by my walk, if not by my talk. The scoffer will go to great lengths in order to observe my life, and even the slightest deviation from the "straight and narrow" immediately raises questions about the credibility of Christ.

It is so tempting to try to "roost" where we can enjoy the best part of both worlds, but God has no neutral zone. While it is certainly not necessary to go around "crowing" about Christianity, we should walk and talk in such a way that we are easily identified as being of the "household of faith." "And do not be conformed to this world, but be transformed by the renewing of your mind, that you may prove what the will of God is, that which is good and acceptable and perfect" (Romans 12:2).

15. DIET RIGHT?

Like newborn babes, long for the pure milk of the word, that by it you may grow in respect to salvation (1 Peter 2:2).

If you've never handled a herd of preschoolers stampeding at the supper table, I doubt whether you can appreciate the following snatches of mealtime conversation:

"I don't want no gravy."

"I want gravy and no potatoes."

"Somebody spilled my milk. There's a puddle under the table."

"What are *you* doing under the table?"

"I'm trying to get out to go to the bathroom."

"She only goes so you won't pass her the vegebubbles."

"Who is ready for dessert?"

"We are!"

"Who wants pumpkin pie and who wants strawberries?"

"I want strawberries on my punkin pie."

And then that profound observation: "Mommy can't have any dessert. She hasn't even finished her soup."

It's little wonder young mothers are pale and irritable. They suffer from malnutrition aggravated by fatigue. The constant interruptions, the endless questions, and the annoying little habits that plague us are all part of raising a family. It can be an overwhelming feeling, and we need time apart to rekindle our energy.

With all the demands upon us, however, we may feel guilty about eating our "dessert" before finishing our "soup," about allowing ourselves some free time to pursue a favorite pastime when there is so much work to be done.

Should I really leave the dishes to soak while I take a brisk walk in the morning sunshine? Do I dare take half an hour to thumb through a favorite magazine? If I do, I discover that life takes on a wider perspective. For one thing, I have something to think about while completing those humdrum little tasks that get me down. I am no longer restricted to my own narrow world.

The same can be said of our spiritual walk. We can be so involved in practical good deeds, it is easy to justify our neglect of the Word. Should I really leave such a cluttered house in order to attend Bible study? If I pause now for personal devotions, will I be able to get lunch ready on time?

Like Martha, we become anxious and troubled, "worried and bothered about so many things" (Luke 10:41*b*). If it is at the expense of our personal and spiritual growth, we need to examine our priorities. Jesus pointed to Mary as the one who wisely took time out to sit at His feet and hear His words.

16. THE LAW OF SUPPLY AND DEMAND

Do not say to your neighbor, "Go and come back, and tomorrow I will give it," when you have it with you (Proverbs 3:28).

We live in a great neighborhood. At any hour of the day or evening, someone is apt to send out an SOS: "Say, I'm baking a cake for the birthday party tomorrow and I ran out of baking powder. I'll send Johnny over for some. OK?"

"Good. That'll be even up for half a cup of cornstarch for my pudding."

We swap everything: cucumbers for carrots, sealer rings for syrup, even tomato soup for toilet tissue.

The only one who complains is the good-natured delivery man when we give him the runaround. He came puffing along yesterday, nearly stepping on his tongue.

"Your neighbor wanted this parcel delivered. Wasn't home. Note said to go to brown house. [Gasp.] Wasn't home either. Note said to leave it here."

"Fine. How much do I owe you?"

"Eighteen dollars and three cents."

"OK, but I'll have to borrow the money from the girl across the street. Here, have a cinnamon bun while you wait." (I figure I have to compensate the fellow somehow.)

I come back to find him talking on my phone. Somebody a few houses over has seen his delivery van and wants to return something. He grabs the cinnamon bun on the way out. "You women ought to run a co-op!"

We do, in a way. Everybody contributes and everybody

shares. The dividend is neighborliness. You can't buy it for a million dollars.

Like any other relationship, however, neighborliness must be based on mutual understanding and respect.

The words *friend* and *neighbor* appear to be interchangeable in the Scriptures, probably because people at that time were more dependent upon one another, and friendships developed naturally. Today we feel very self-sufficient, quite capable of managing our own lives without the help of neighbors. Are we then justified in ignoring them?

If we do, we miss the opportunity of cultivating valuable friendships right at our doorstep. That in itself is a priceless privilege, but it is also a most effective way of curbing misunderstandings. Once we learn how others feel, we can also learn how to avoid unnecessary friction. More than that, we are able to communicate the Gospel in everyday terms.

Once mutual trust is established, neighborliness just naturally develops. It is a code of ethics based on Romans 13:10, "Love does no wrong to a neighbor; love therefore is the fulfillment of the law."

17. CHICKEN POPS

As one whom his mother comforts, so I will comfort you (Isaiah 66:13a).

I hear someone shuffling up to my bedside in the dark. A small voice whimpers, "I don't feel so good."

I stumble out of bed and follow the patter of little feet into the bathroom. The patient squints up at me as I switch on the light. Her face is covered with bright red polka dots. I hustle her back to bed.

"What's she got?" friend hubby mumbles in his sleep.

"I don't know, but she's covered with more dots than a yard of Swiss organdy."

"Must be chicken pox."

It is. She greets the news with mixed emotions. Being sick means you can stay home from school, have breakfast in bed, and watch TV.

It also means you miss your part in the school play, you don't feel like eating in the first place, and you discover a mother is poor company compared to playmates. Very poor indeed.

She would have been bored to death had it not been for the antics of Purrvess the tomcat. He meanders into her bedroom first thing in the morning and peers into her face with large inquisitive eyes. She giggles.

With typical feline curiosity, Dr. Purrvess diagnoses the case. His whiskers tickle. She giggles some more.

A freeloader by nature, he eyes the patient's breakfast.

I go to tend to details in the kitchen.

"Mom! Come quick! The cat's drinking my milk!"

I go to investigate. There is a mysterious lump under the covers. It purrs.

The patient looks sheepish. "Mom, do cats ever get the chicken pops?"

Like the tomcat, we sometimes push our interests into matters which are ordinarily off limits to us as Christians. Sometimes God even allows us to taste of the "forbidden fruit," not that He wants to punish us, but that we might learn from experience.

Plagued by guilt feelings, we may feel God is withholding His comforting hand. Instead, He is hiding us close to Himself, much like our little girl with her pet cat. He knows what it is like to suffer, and He is concerned about us not just for the moment but for our entire life. "For momentary light affliction is producing for us an eternal weight of glory far beyond all comparison" (2 Corinthians 4:17).

18. ALL-AMERICAN TAILOR

*There is neither Jew nor Greek, there is neither slave
nor free man, there is neither male nor female, for you
are all one in Christ Jesus* (Galatians 3:28).

I innocently offer my limited talents to the local school,
and without knowing it, I am labeled as a "resource person."

Don't be fooled by the handle. It just means I am to help
a grade-two class with a sewing project.

Armed with needles, thread, and scissors, I set foot within those hallowed halls of learning, unaware that I am about
to be instrumental in producing the outstanding tailor of
all time.

He is a freckle-faced, towheaded young rascal who has
been conditioned to resent anything that even faintly
resembles femininity.

I thread his needle.

"I don't wanna thew." He sits with his arms crossed and
his feet hooked around his chair legs. "That'th girl thtuff."

"You like football better?"

Now we're talking! I tell him about seeing the picture
of the quarterback who sews for a hobby. "Why, he even
won first prize in a sewing contest competing with over 200
women!"

"You mean that?" My prodigy peers up at me through
horn-rimmed glasses.

I assure him it's true and move on.

I am in the midst of helping a whole group of children
untangle their knots when our young tackle comes charging

42

through the huddle, kicking the competitor for my attention in the shins as he does so.

"Look at thith, Mrs. Barkman! Ain't that good!"

I assure him it's excellent. (Under the circumstances, of course.)

"Boy, oh boy! I'm gonna be a thuper thtar thewer!" He heads back to his desk, elated by his achievement.

I don't suppose that lisp will be any great drawback in the long run. He's already hurdled the worst handicap— the preconceived notion that some things in life are sissy stuff.

In Western culture there seems to be a stigma attached to those hobbies or occupations that are primarily done by women. Teased unmercifully by his peers, a small boy quickly smothers any artistic or musical talent he may possess. It's just too embarrassing to intrude into an area labeled "for women only" unless he is strong enough to withstand the ridicule involved.

I'm afraid the same concept applies to religion. Men have been led to believe that faith is a crutch for women and children, but certainly not necessary for the "all-American male." They are thus caught between social pressure and their own spiritual longings.

As mothers, I believe we should reassure our sons that their manhood is not the absence of tenderness, but the fulfillment of strength—physical, moral, and spiritual. Gifts and talents are intended to complement God's divine purpose "until we all attain to the unity of the faith, and of the knowledge of the Son of God, to a mature man, to the measure of the stature which belongs to the fulness of Christ" (Ephesians 4:13).

19. RUBBER SNAKES

Behold, I send you out as sheep in the midst of wolves;
therefore be shrewd as serpents, and innocent as doves
(Matthew 10:16).

Every so often we conscript Grandma to baby-sit, so she
loads up her suitcase with headache pills and nerve tonic
and hikes a ride in from the country on the nearest bus line.

Her visit casts a magic spell upon the young fry. Cheeks
bulge mysteriously between meals, and appetites wane accordingly. As the supply of candy dwindles, she expresses a
desire to do some shopping. "Let me take the kids along.
They'll be no trouble at all."

Envisioning the weekend crowds thronging the shopping
center, I am reluctant to grant her wish. "Well—if you
insist."

They troop off happily, chattering to Grandma as they go.

Considering the length of the shopping list, they are back
relatively soon.

"Did you manage to get through the crowds OK?"

"Oh, sure! No trouble at all!"

"That's cuz we have a secret!" The boy pulls a rubber
snake from his pocket. I shrink back in horror.

"Wherever did you get that thing?"

"Grandma bought it for me. Said I could play with it
while we shopped. The ladies didn't like it much. They always backed away, and we got waited on first sometimes."

Grandma quickly comes to his defense. "Land sakes, anybody who is brave enough to cope with that city traffic
shouldn't be afraid of a little old rubber snake!"

It's true, of course, but it is also typical of human nature to react defensively when suddenly confronted by the unfamiliar.

I personally fear any number of "rubber snakes"—situations from which I instinctively pull back. Sometimes it's social pressure or meeting new people or venturing into strange places. Feelings of inadequacy cause me to linger behind when I should forge ahead confidently.

On the other hand, I rush headlong into situations that I am sure would make angels tremble; yet, there I am, sublimely unaware of any consequences.

Fear of the unknown may hold its share of imaginary rubber snakes, but contempt for the familiar exposes us to the very real danger of dropping our defenses. We need grace and wisdom to distinguish between the harmless and the harmful. "Be of sober spirit, be on the alert. Your adversary, the devil, prowls about like a roaring lion, seeking someone to devour" (1 Peter 5:8).

20. MANY INGREDIENTS, ONE RECIPE

Then Elijah said to her, ". . . make me a little bread cake from it first, and bring it out to me, and afterward you may make one for yourself and for your son" (1 Kings 17:13).

Whenever I bake fruitcake, the five-year-old pulls up his chair. "What are those things?"

"Cherries for the cake."

"I'll pick out the green ones. They aren't ripe yet, are they, Mom?" (I hadn't thought of that one before.)

"Why are you using old raisins?"

"What do you mean, 'old raisins'?"

"They're all wrinkled up, like Grandma. What's in *that* box?"

"Baking soda."

"It comes from a cow, right?"

"No. Why?"

"Cuz there's a cow on the box. Hey, don't put that stuff in the cake! The man on TV says it's for the kitty's box so it won't smell."

I explain that baking soda has more than one use. Like milk, for instance.

"Milk comes for a cow, too. Like soda. Right, Mom?"

Talk about misleading labels! I stir the fruit and nuts into the batter. My helper turns up his nose. "That looks like when I threw up."

"Mm, but it smells good."

He takes a cautious whiff. "Yeah, but it still looks awful."

"Oh, but the proof of the pudding is in the eating," I tell him.

He looks puzzled. "You said you were baking cake, not pudding."

"Look, I'll just give you a piece later. How's that?"

He skips happily away.

I am sure as that son grows older, he will be much more hesitant to accept my word for anything. He will be anxious to test and try many different claims before coming to a decision, particularly in matters pertaining to the faith.

In his search for truth, he will probably be somewhat confused by "misleading labels," sometimes through his own misunderstanding, sometimes because of the variety of spiritual gifts, occasionally through people deliberately trying to lead him astray.

As the batter bears little resemblance to the finished cake, however, he will have to judge for himself, not on the basis of initial appearance, but on those deeper qualities of love, trust, and obedience to God.

I hope he discovers through personal commitment to Christ the truth of Psalm 34:8, "O taste and see that the LORD is good; how blessed is the man who takes refuge in Him."

21. STRIPPED OF OUR COSTUME

The Lord is my light and my salvation; whom shall I fear? (Psalm 27:1a).

A certain haunting atmosphere prevails over the house at this time of year. Dried leaves rattling against the windowpane keep reminding me of a skeleton in the closet. I imagine bats fluttering about the attic, their flight patterns distorted by the cobwebs draped from the rafters.

Even the old tomcat acts strange. Of late he's been keeping close vigil on the broom, eyeing it as a potential spacecraft. Last year he persisted in using the jack-o'-lantern as a launching pad. If his tail ever catches fire he won't wait for the countdown, I can assure you.

Overactive imaginations at this time of year mean only one thing—Halloween. Who can remain perfectly aloof with all those little ghosts and goblins getting ready to besiege you for tricks and treats?

Yesterday the two smallest children were rummaging through a box in search of appropriate attire for spooks. During the process one turned to the other and said, "I will get in a costume, and you will get in a costume, and then we will be afraid of ourselves!"

For many of us, such fears are far too realistic as it is! Imagining that we may not be accepted the way we are, we masquerade under all sorts of disguises in order to fit the occasion. If extended over a long period of time, such pretense eventually masks our true identity, and we no longer recognize what God intended us to be.

From time to time it is wise to ask ourselves these questions: What image do I portray? Is it what I really am? If not, why am I doing it? Do I fear rejection? Is it pride? Am I afraid someone will one day poke a hole in my "costume" and discover the real me?

Honest answers to such questions can change our whole outlook on life. We should be ourselves, and, with the grace of God, we should strive to be all we're meant to be. Fears and insecurity can only be eliminated, however, by bringing them out into the open, not hiding them beneath a cloak of "let's pretend."

Even staunch old Joshua had his times of misgiving, but he assumed command of the situation by claiming the same promise available to us today: "'Have I not commanded you? Be strong and courageous! Do not tremble or be dismayed, for the LORD your God is with you wherever you go'" (Joshua 1:9).

22. FIRSTFRUITS OR LEFTOVERS?

*For I was hungry, and you gave Me something to eat;
I was thirsty, and you gave Me drink* (Matthew 25:35a).

Every time I see somebody board the bus with a battered old lunch pail under his arm it evokes a wave of sympathy for people who have to carry their lunch to work day after day. No doubt the contents and container have both improved greatly since I went to school, but I still equate lunch pails with tinny-tasting sandwiches and bruised apples.

It was a long way to school in those days, and for some reason the lunch pails always bore the brunt of the jostling. On more than one occasion I opened my lunch pail to discover my cheese sandwiches floating in cocoa brown sludge—the cork had popped out of my thermos.

I was never too fond of cocoa to begin with, but I spent an anxious morning wondering if any more sandwiches would be forthcoming. School pals were always most generous, pawning off what they didn't like anyway to victims of such disasters.

Incidentally, I always had a hard time convincing my mother that tomato sandwiches made poor traveling companions. They not only made the bread soggy, but they developed a peculiar stale taste the minute they hit the lunch pail. After about five years of trial and error, I settled down to cheese sandwiches—five days a week, forty weeks a year.

It sounds like a very humdrum diet in terms of today's menu, but it was nutritious and filling. If I protested now and then, I was told that I should be grateful. Millions of kids in the world didn't have a lunch to take, let alone a lunch pail to put it in. The same holds true today, so who are we to complain? Yet we spend millions of dollars each year catering to the whims of our appetites.

Sandwiched somewhere between the junk foods and the gourmet ingredients is a balanced diet, if we would only be satisfied with it. Unfortunately, we tend to overlook what we *need* in favor of what we *want*. The results are not only devastating in terms of health, but also disastrous to the pocketbook. Unable to stay within our own food budget, we haven't so much as leftovers to share with the starving.

I believe my stewardship as a homemaker is not restricted to that portion of money that goes toward the church. Stewardship encompasses a much wider scope, including economical, nutritious cooking and less waste of food. My conscience is not comfortable catering to whims and fancies, because I believe that we, as Christians, have a deeper responsibility to the world food problem.

If God favors us with peace of mind, is it asking too much to favor Him with a piece of bread, given in His name? "Cast your bread on the surface of the waters, for you will find it after many days. Divide your portion to seven, or even to eight, for you do not know what misfortune may occur on the earth" (Ecclesiastes 11:1-2).

23. LOVE IS CONTAGIOUS

It is good not to eat meat or to drink wine, or to do anything by which your brother stumbles (Romans 14: 21).

When the flu bug strikes this household, we hit the bed like dominoes.

First one down is the girl in grade one. She comes home at noon with bleary red eyes. "I don't feel good." Up comes her breakfast, just like that. She staggers off to bed.

Close on her heels is the fellow in kindergarten. He takes one sip of soup and begins to green around the gills. "I wanna go to bed."

Next one home is the fellow in grade nine. "I'm not hungry today." (That's certainly a new twist!)

All afternoon I am busy tending to emergency measures. At last friend hubby comes home from work. He promptly keels over on the bed. That's four down and two to go, not counting the cat.

"What can you people eat for supper?" I go around and collect orders. Just then the oldest teenager arrives home from work, still hale and hearty.

"Supper? Oh, I'll just make myself a Dagwood sandwich. Let's see now—pickles, cheese, olives, tomatoes, lettuce, salami—"

The supper trays look grim in comparison: half a cracker, black tea, dry bread.

"Cancel my order" comes a feeble plea from the back bedroom. "The smell of that salami is killing me."

In deference to the victim's wishes, we close his bedroom door. It's the very least we can do under the circumstances.

Without really being aware of it, I feel that many times we thoughtlessly flaunt our good health or possessions or even our spiritual insights in front of those who are unable to bear up under the comparison. Those who are sensitive about their failing health may not really appreciate us talking about the many miles we jog.

People struggling to make ends meet probably feel left out as they listen to us ramble on and on about our latest vacation.

The Christian who has not grown spiritually may shrink back even further when confronted by someone with deeper insight and wider knowledge of the Bible.

While there is certainly nothing wrong with discussing health or family vacations or sharing spiritual insights, we should try to view life through the other person's circumstances and adapt our conversation or actions accordingly. It is but one small way in which we can show genuine concern.

"Now we who are strong ought to bear the weaknesses of those without strength and not just please ourselves" (Romans 15:1).

24. IF IT WEREN'T FOR GRANDMA!

Her children rise up and bless her (Proverbs 31:28*a*).

Sometimes I would really like to get away from it all. Hire a cook, a cleaning lady, a laundry maid, a baby-sitter, a chauffeur, a secretary, and a bookkeeper; then pack my bags and take off. As you can see, it's not quite that simple.

The cook, unless she's a very stouthearted sort, would probably blanch at the amount of food two teenage boys can devour at one sitting, let alone the rest of the family. I've long since learned to scoff at the proportions of a recipe that says "serves six." I just double it by instinct and hope the food will stretch to the end of the appetites.

A genuine cleaning lady would probably take strong exception to the smudges on the wall. If at first she didn't notice them, it's because the dust is so thick on the light fixtures. And should she decide to clean the closets, I hope she outruns the avalanche that threatens anyone who opens my sewing cupboard.

I'm sure the laundry maid would have trouble with lint adhering to the corduroy pants. That's because two boys are left-handed and she would instinctively look in the wrong (right) pocket for their used hankies. I can't believe that she could learn in a week what has taken me fifteen years of disciplined practice to master.

Just when the baby-sitter is anticipating a few minutes respite from her duties, a conscientious little mother will hand her a raggedy old teddy bear, pleading her case ever so eloquently. "Teddy has no pajamas, and he gets cold, and he needs a hat and some socks and a—." Unless she's a capable seamstress, the baby-sitter had better beware about making any rash promises.

Likewise the chauffeur. Pick one son up, drop one son off, haul the groceries home, pick second son up, drop neighbor's kids off at pool, pick first son up. Some days it takes a computerized time table. On other days the car won't start.

That's where the secretary comes in. Make phone calls, take phone calls, relay messages, type business letters, pay bills. Better check with the bookkeeper first. The checks might bounce.

As I say, sometimes I would really like to get away from it all, if only I could integrate matters. The kids have the perfect solution: "Just invite Grandma in to stay with us! She's got lots of experience! Even more than you, Mom."

A grandmother is what you call a natural asset, a built-in blessing to a growing family. Do we make her feel *wanted?* Or does she feel *used?* Most grandmothers have lived a long and busy life, and the desire to remain useful constitutes a very real need. Some families, however, tend to take unfair advantage of her baby-sitting services to the point where she no longer appreciates it.

Other families disregard Grandma as being incapable of coping with a lively brood. She is thus deprived of the pleasure, and in her old age she feels empty and forsaken. Many factors are to be considered, of course, but we should not knowingly deny Grandmother the privilege of making a very unique contribution to family life. "He makes the barren woman abide in the house as a joyful mother of children. Praise the LORD!" (Psalm 113:9).

55

25. FULL LOADS, EMPTY POCKETS

Let your clothes be white all the time (Ecclesiastes 9:
8a).

Every time I do the laundry, I think back to the days when
we had to melt snow for washday. The copper boiler on top
of the old wood stove sputtered and rocked in protest as
Mother stoked up the fire. Those old kitchens were not too
warm to begin with, and all those tubs full of snow certainly
did nothing to raise the temperature of the room.

It seemed to me that I would have just nicely thawed out
when it was time to bring in a line full of frozen wash.
Fleece-lined suits of underwear had a habit of freezing into
grotesque shapes, and we kids used to have great fun match-
ing them up to local personalities. Draped over the wooden
clotheshorse, they gradually assumed their conventional
shape, a chilling rebuke to our active imaginations.

Despite modern conveniences, some aspects of laundry
day never change. You still need a clothespin on your nose
when you peel apart the teenager's socks. And kids still leave
all sorts of junk in their pockets, to be claimed long after
the trinkets have disintegrated in the wash and the papers
have plugged the lint trap.

And in their work pants, husbands still carry nails and
the wing nut from last year's lawn mower as well as springs
and sprockets from various machines—all sorts of me-
chanical equipment they never use but are loath to part with.
"I might need it sometime. Be sure you keep it!" I have a
collection down there that fills a three-pound pail.

I am also expert at patching pockets.

As I mend the holes and reinforce the seams, I am reminded of all the worries, fears, anxieties, and doubts we carry around from week to week without really noticing them. Suddenly the accumulated weight becomes too much, and we break under the strain.

We need to develop the habit of emptying our pockets, so to speak. We must spread out our feelings before the Lord, prayerfully sort things through, and ask Him to dispose of the trash. In so doing, we will discover that we have exchanged our "spirit of heaviness" for a "garment of praise" (Isaiah 61:3, KJV*).

*King James Version.

26. A LOWLY TOP EXECUTIVE

Walk in a manner worthy of the calling with which you have been called, with all humility and gentleness, with patience, showing forbearance to one another in love (Ephesians 4:1b-2).

I am shuffling around in my housecoat when I hear the familiar clank. The garbage is being collected, and our weekly accumulation is buried somewhere under a snowdrift at the back door.

Unable to loosen the entire can, I pry off the lid, grab the contents, and head down the driveway, still wearing my housecoat.

I arrive just in time to be greeted by the garbage man.

"Say, ma'am, you shouldn't oughta be out here like that. Gonna catch a death of a cold. But never mind. I won't tell a soul you slept in."

Bless his heart! During spring the garbage cans stick to the mud like suction cups, but he never misses a single one, slogging through the puddles with the patience of Job.

In summer the contents stand for hours in the heat of the noonday sun, but I have yet to see him flinch when he removes the lid.

Last fall I thought I would do him a favor and tote the garbage across the road to his truck. I was just about to hand it to him when the bag broke. Not the least bit daunted, he scooped up the wilted potato peelings and the chewed-over corncobs, brushed off his gloves, and said, "Don't feel bad, ma'am. What's a few leftovers between friends?"

In my opinion, that garbage collector is walking worthy

of his "vocation"—no self-pity, no complaints about the lowliness of his job, no loss of self-worth.

I wonder what my attitude would be in his position? I am afraid I would not show the same tact and friendliness as he displayed when faced with such disagreeable conditions.

Do we look with less regard upon people holding menial jobs? Do we consider our own work as somewhat beneath our dignity? Remember that, from God's viewpoint, the "top executive" may be a garbage collector who willingly and cheerfully performs his duties, a "laborer . . . worthy of his wages" (1 Timothy 5:18*b*).

27. SILENCE IS GOLDEN

*The words of the wise heard in quietness are better than
the shouting of a ruler among fools* (Ecclesiastes 9:17).

I have a habit of leaning on my grocery cart and compar-
ing prices at the local supermarket. I suspect, however, that
merchants use background music as a subtle form of brainwashing. Just when I am about to make some monumental
decision regarding the best buy in crackers, the 101 Strings
start playing "Seventy-six Trombones" and spoil my arithme-
tic. What were those prices again? Oh, skip it. I'll just
grab a box and keep going. It turns out to be the most expensive brand. See what I mean about brainwashing?

You've probably noticed that background music is never
loud and distinct. It just drones away incessantly in the
dark recesses of the subconscious like a lone mosquito on a
summer's night. Just when you're least prepared, it zeros
in for the kill.

Say I am waiting for a doctor's appointment, doubled
over with pain. Suddenly it strikes me: that's the Boston
Pops performing "Mack the Knife." Some nurse even has
the gall to hum along. I clutch my sides as panic sends fresh
waves of pain across my innards. Who said background
music is relaxing? Just once I wish a sympathetic doctor
would prescribe complete silence so I could suffer in peace
and quiet.

And then there is that old fallacy about good music being
conducive to stimulating conversation. It's stimulating, all
right. Spend an evening competing with a stereo, and the
volume reaches such proportions that I feel I'm involved in

a shouting match. What ever happened to a "quiet evening with friends"?

For that matter, what ever became of quiet times anywhere? Whenever we enter a room, the first thing we do is switch on the radio or TV. We install tape decks in our cars, we pipe music into our stores, and we drag along transistors wherever we go. Little wonder that silent meditation is almost a thing of the past.

Perhaps it's time we acknowledged the fact that we can no longer live with our own thoughts, nor are we willing to try. Consequently, we do not allow the still, small voice of God to penetrate our lives and exercise the same degrees of influence that it once did. We are, in effect, expecting God to shout out His orders above and beyond the noise of the world.

God is worthy of quiet reverence. "Let the words of my mouth and the meditation of my heart be acceptable in Thy sight, O LORD, my rock and my redeemer" (Psalm 19:14).

28. DRESS ACCORDINGLY

Thou dost enlarge my steps under me, and my feet have not slipped (2 Samuel 22:37).

Here on the Canadian prairies it takes a hardy constitution to withstand Christmas shopping. Bundled up against the bone-chilling temperatures, even the fleet-footed are seriously handicapped. Wearing all five sweaters, I can't possibly put my arms down at my sides where they belong. As a result, I go waddling along penguin-style, with arms extended like a pair of flippers.

A neighbor of ours has similar problems. Instead of five sweaters, she wears two pair of her hubby's thermal drawers. Even without the handicap of sweaters, she has trouble keeping up to his manly strides.

Enroute to a distant bargain counter last winter, she was holding fast to her husband's hand, consequently missing every second or third step as he sped along at top shopping speed. As if that and dodging the crowds were not enough already, our friend's problems were compounded by a further predicament. The thermal drawers slid down. Not quite to her feet, but far enough to make an effective hobble. She ducked into an obscure corner and discreetly pulled them up again, only to have history repeat itself every few minutes.

By now her suspicious actions alerted a clerk who was about ready to escort her to the office on a charge of shoplifting had not hubby intervened. More annoyed than embarrassed, her hubby suggested that she go and buy a good pair of suspenders.

To brace ourselves for the unexpected is to exercise wisdom. As Christians, we know where we are going and our arrival in heaven is assured. But are we prepared to cope with the emergencies along the way?

In Ephesians 6 we are reminded of the spiritual forces of wickedness that try to hinder our progress. Paul refers to it as warfare and admonishes us to put on the whole "armor of God" as protection from the onslaughts of the enemy.

Now, our concept of armor is that of rigid, heavy, and uncomfortable steel that refuses to yield either to us or to the enemy. God's armor, being far more adaptable, is much more effective. Truth, righteousness, peace, faith, salvation, His Word, prayer—are these not more appealing than actual breastplates, girdles, shields, helmets, and swords? When we avail ourselves of God's armor, we are suitably attired for whatever comes our way. "Therefore, take up the full armor of God, that you may be able to resist in the evil day, and having done everything, to stand firm"(Ephesians 6:13).

29. CHASING THE PAST

After whom are you pursuing? After a dead dog, after a single flea? (1 Samuel 24:14*b*).

A certain elderly pooch had been left with a neighbor while its rightful owner was away on holidays. The shock of boarding out proved to be too much for the old dog's constitution, and the woman told me she got up one morning and found him dead under the kitchen table.

In a big city, giving away a live dog is difficult enough, but whatever would she do with a canine carcass? After numerous phone calls and several futile attempts to dispose of it, her only recourse seemed to be the local humane society. They agreed to arrange a burial if she would bring the remains to their headquarters.

Since the woman had to go there by bus, transporting the body posed something of a problem. After considering the various alternatives, she decided to put the expired dog in an old suitcase and simply carry him to his final resting place, while still maintaining a maximum degree of dignity.

Halfway to her destination, she had to change buses, and some fellow very graciously offered to carry her piece of luggage. He murmured something about its being a dead weight, and when she refused to divulge the contents, he must have concluded she was smuggling gold. At any rate, she boarded the next bus and looked back just in time to see the culprit absconding down a back alley with the suitcase. Her first impulse was to give chase; but then, like David of old, she was struck by the absurdity of the situation. Chasing a dead dog, of all things! With that, she settled back to enjoy the ride home, mission accomplished.

In the spiritual sense, the Lord expects us to do the same, yet we sometimes insist on chasing down "back alleys" in a vain attempt to recapture part of the past, robbed from us by time.

The former beauty queen, for instance, looks in the mirror, searching for the points that helped her win the contest many years before.

The businessman tries to retrace his decisions, hoping to expand his company in a different direction this time around.

The athlete of bygone days works out against the clock and the dreams of recapturing the title jogging his memory.

A mother looks upon her growing children with dismay, and her maternal arms ache with emptiness.

As difficult as it is to accept, all of the past is history. Any efforts toward actually reliving certain periods of our lives are but absurd attempts to regain what is gone forever. Such efforts would be a worthless pursuit of time, energy, and money. In contrast, the Christian faith enables us to learn from the past, apply it to the present, and hope for the future. Instead of chasing dead dogs down dark alleys, our walk should illustrate Proverbs 4:18, "But the path of the righteous is like the light of dawn, that shines brighter and brighter until the full day."

30. THE WARM COMFORTER OF ASSURANCE

The bed is too short on which to stretch out, and the blanket is too small to wrap oneself in (Isaiah 28:20).

It's the time of year we dig out our hobbies to ward off the midwinter blues. For some time I had threatened to claim a corner of the rec room for my own particular pursuit. Our teenagers paid no heed. At last I just gathered up my quilting frames and barged in.

"Good grief! She's even armed! We knew you were old, Mom, but do you have to resort to a battering ram?"

Oblivious to their comments, I proceeded to set up my quilt. They retreated to their corner, grumbling something about democracy being overtaken by a dictatorship. Female at that.

I had counted on some opposition from the kids, but I hadn't taken the tomcat into consideration. He has a certain insecurity when ignored, and his inner anxiety manifests itself in very vocal protests. Every time I went downstairs to quilt, he apparently felt abandoned, and pitiful yowls grated upon my conscience.

One afternoon when he was meandering around in his usual state of self-pity, he stumbled upon me and my quilt. Forsooth! This was indeed a new endeavor, and his feline curiosity literally knew no bounds. He pounced up beside me and proceeded to investigate my quilting technique at close range.

Obviously fascinated, he could not help but become involved. A paw here, a claw there, and my nerves were soon in knots, never mind the thread!

Determined to finish, I stitched relentlessly on over a period of days, with the teenagers undermining my efforts by their snide remarks and the tomcat counteracting my every move. Wouldn't you know it? When the quilt was finished, the teenagers squabbled over who would sleep under it, the tomcat claimed it for his own, and I was left out in the cold.

Now, nothing hinders a good night's sleep like too few covers. First you try rolling yourself into a ball in a vain attempt to keep warm. Then you start getting cramps in your legs. You straighten out your legs, and your feet get cold. You pull the covers down over your feet, and your shoulders are bare. By this time you are wide awake, with little to do but lie there in the cold, dark night and listen to your teeth chatter.

The person who tries to rest in his own good works experiences much the same frustrations. At first she may try to justify herself by saying, "I'm just as good as Jane. Why worry?" Before long she observes Jane's standards are considerably lower than her own. Then she tries to console herself the other way by saying, "At least I'm better than Jane!"

Somehow she is not too comfortable with that idea either. What she would really like to know is how she measures up before *God*. But she goes along doing the best she can, her soul tossing and turning as if in fitful sleep, her conscience ever alert to the slightest accusation. What the poor woman needs is a "good night's rest." She should forget the idea that she must work her way into heaven, and instead, simply entrust her life to the Savior. "How blessed is he whose transgression is forgiven, whose sin is *covered!*" (Psalm 32:1, italics added.)

31. WEATHERWISE

Hast thou entered into the treasures of the snow? (Job 38:22a, KJV).

At a time when the northern prairies were grinding and squeaking their way through a typical Canadian winter, we had occasion to visit Canada's west coast for a weekend.

I was not too impressed and made the mistake of saying so. I received a letter forthwith from an irate young lady in Vancouver who took me to task for criticizing their wet weather. She went on at length to point out the geophysical necessity of rainfall along the west coast and ended her geography lesson with a stinging rebuke about my failure to appreciate the finer aspects of God's great creation.

Maybe so. On the other hand, I've always suspected that when God finished with the west coast, He moved on inland to something more challenging. Any old clod has to admire the rugged grandeur and majestic beauty of mountain scenery. It takes a real connoisseur of art, however, to crawl out of bed at thirty-two degrees below zero and appreciate the exquisite handiwork of the Almighty on the frosted windowpane. But when the sun starts bouncing off a million diamonds in the snow, you don't even yearn to see your reflection in the mud puddles of warmer climates.

And nothing is quite so exhilarating as pushing your wealthy neighbor out of a snowdrift and realizing that Cadillacs have square tires, too, come January. Up to now you always felt a little self-conscious about thumping past his mansion at forty below in your little compact. But, rich or poor, you are simply one against the elements, as any blizzard verifies. When the first south wind starts nibbling at the snowbanks around about March, however, the tingle of excitement you experience has no equal. Spring fever is one of the more delightful compensations afforded prairie dwellers.

Just as a person from the tropics could not possibly enjoy our Canadian winter until he becomes acclimatized to it, so the "natural man does not accept the things of the Spirit of God; for they are foolishness to him, and he cannot understand them, because they are spiritually appraised" (1 Corinthians 2:14). If, however, we are willing to accept the challenge of the gospel and adapt our lives accordingly, we gain a new appreciation for the Scriptures.

Some passages we discover will delight our souls with their beauty and depth. From the ''mountaintop'' to the "valley" the view will be decidedly different, yet unique in its own way.

Unless we're widely traveled we cannot comprehend, much less appreciate, all the various aspects of climate throughout the world, nor can we ever fully understand *every* passage of Scripture. If we can't appreciate the "snowdrifts," we should at least pause to enjoy the "snowflakes," those intricate truths in God's Word, which fall gently down upon the heart and melt into the soul.

32. SENSITIVITY AWARENESS

Who can understand his errors? Cleanse thou me from secret faults (Psalm 19:12, KJV).

They came home from school day after day, clutching the fruits of their labor in sweaty little hands. "One apple and two apples make three apples. Pear starts with a *p*. A banana is yellow."

They are so proud of their efforts that you must *never* destroy their initiative by ignoring their school papers. So you admire the neat (?) printing, marvel at the gold star, and encourage their artistic endeavors by agreeing that a green squirrel really does look more becoming than a plain brown one.

And then you wonder what to do with all those papers.

Temporarily you'll just put them here on the cupboard where Daddy will see them. Tomorrow you might be able to slip them into the paper stand. The day after that is garbage pickup—

"Hey, Mommy! Don't throw away my good papers! I want to keep them!"

"Oh, I didn't realize."

"And they're all wrinkled up!"

"Don't cry, dear. We'll put them here on the cupboard, and when I iron, I'll press them all out nice and smooth again."

"Really?"

"Really. And then you find a nice place for them in your room, OK?"

So you press them all out and get crayon stuck to your

iron, and Junior promptly takes them and scrunches them into an overcrowded desk and forgets about them.

A year later when you're doing spring cleaning and everybody's gone so there are no witnesses to the crime, you take a big black plastic bag that won't betray your foul deed and you empty Junior's desk.

We do many things in the course of a lifetime that, while not necessarily wrong, are nevertheless painful to other people. Dismissing as frivolous what others might consider precious, substituting the practical for the sentimental, failing to appreciate the full significance of a gift—these are but a few areas in which we hurt others. Our reaction may not be intentional, but that does not prevent the other person from taking offense.

Regardless of how differently we look at things as individuals, we must respect the feelings of those around us. It is all too easy to convince ourselves that our methods or our values or our concepts are the only valid choices that exist.

Even though he was a great man of God, King David wisely prayed, "Keep back Thy servant from presumptuous sins; let them not rule over me" (Psalm 19:13a).

33.   BUDGET BLUES?

Give me neither poverty nor riches; feed me with the food that is my portion" (Proverbs 30:8).

I picked up a newspaper the other day and saw that, according to the latest statistics, our family has just pulled out of the poverty level. I had never realized our financial state of affairs was so poor.

True, the kids are wearing jeans with holes in the knees, but that's by choice, not necessity. Contrary to popular opinion, I do own two pairs of shoes, but these bedraggled, old bedroom slippers are simply the ultimate in comfort. And that old hat my husband wears is just an excuse. He claims the new styles don't do him justice. Maybe it's just as well. He's worn the old one so long that if he were to replace it, the assessment officials might consider it a local improvement and raise the property tax. Now that I know we're scraping along just above the poverty level, I dare say we could ill afford the extra burden.

In spite of what statistics say, we aren't forced to do without clothes, we enjoy three square meals a day, and the roof over our head is paid for, even if we shingled it ourselves. After starting with less than forty dollars between us, we thought we were sitting very comfortably. Now, twenty years of marriage, four kids, three cats, two houses, and five cars later, the experts tell me we have only been subsisting. I wonder what *real* living is like?

I realize that for some people in this world, poverty is a stark reality. For others, it's just a state of mind.

How disturbed should we be if our income falls below the

national average, or even below the neighbor's? I am much more concerned about how well we handle our present finances. There is always the possibility that I am poor because I feel poor, not because I lack necessities.

Rather than striving to obtain a better standard of living by simply making more money, perhaps I need to adjust my attitude toward spending. If we are sincerely willing to try to stay within the amounts God has allotted us, I believe He will honor our efficiency.

Now and then it is wise to go over the budget systematically, bearing in mind Solomon's wise advice: "Poor is he who works with a *negligent* hand" (Proverbs 10:4*a*, italics added.)

34.   ADVANCE OR RETREAT?

Hide me from the secret counsel of evildoers, from the tumult of those who do iniquity, who have sharpened their tongue like a sword (Psalm 64:2-3a).

You'd think it was the battle din of the republic. Bit by bit, the teenagers have added to their noisemaking equipment until at present they have something like two stereos, a tape deck, six speakers, an electric piano, a bass guitar, and an amplifier. Plus a piano and synthesizer.

As if that weren't enough, one son very graciously offered to store his friend's set of drums in our rec room, the excuse being that they could practice together.

So now the drums go bang and the cymbals clang and Mother has a perpetual headache.

The kids are having a ball.

I don't mind the racket too much if I'm going at a leisurely pace. I sort of dismiss the whole thing as being a passing phase. I tell myself they'll grow out of it, and the sooner the better.

But when the pressure's on and the time is short, all that noise is nothing short of aggravated assault on the eardrums, a raging pandemonium of decibels designed to brainwash the less obstinate into submission.

I'm stubborn. I may conciliate to some extent, I might even compromise here and there, but I do not intend to vacate the premises.

Meanwhile the battle rages, and I have begun to wonder about who starts a war. Is it really the fellow who fires the first shot? King David seemed very aware that our enemy often aggravates a situation by spreading bitter words behind our backs in order to provoke us to retaliate. Then, when we do, the enemy points an accusing finger and says, "Look what so-and-so did for no reason at all, and she even calls herself a Christian!"

Such experiences can be extremely trying because they stretch our patience to the very breaking point. Instead of beating a hasty retreat, however, we are to stand our ground in love, our very words and actions deflecting any charges which might be hurled against us. "In addition to all, taking up the shield of faith with which you will be able to extinguish all the flaming missiles of the evil one" (Ephesians 6:16).

35. A PLACE IN THE SON

I planted, Apollos watered, but God was causing the growth (1 Corinthians 3:6).

You don't really miss them until you begin to look around for someplace to put the geranium Great-Aunt Matilda gave you. Then you realize that modern houses lack one obvious convenience—windowsills.

In a very limited way, windowsills were substitutes for greenhouses. I say "limited" only in terms of space, because sometime in March, every kind of greenery imaginable began to sprout from the soup cans standing in sunny south windows. If the tomcat became jealous because the plants were usurping his place in the sun, it was just too bad. From March to May the windowsills were off limits to intruders, and he would just have to wait until transplanting time before basking in his favorite spot.

More than once Junior got his seat dusted for poking around in the dwarf marigolds, but in later years he also learned some invaluable lessons in horticulture as he watched the newborn seedlings develop into full-fledged plants.

As time went on, I recall a great deal of chitchat taking place over the merits of growing your own bedding plants as opposed to buying them from commercial greenhouses. I suppose some architect-type fellow eventually became jealous of his wife's green thumb and tried to put a stop to it once and for all by designing windows with no sills. He may have curtailed matters somewhat, but the more enthusiastic get around the inconvenience very nicely. They just set their

TV trays in front of a south picture window and grow greenery to their pocketbook's content.

Bighearted folks that they are, they even slip the rest of us a handout now and then in the form of surplus bedding plants. I, for one, appreciate their generosity. Theirs is the gift that grows. It is to be hoped.

I would hate to disappoint those people who helped get my garden off to a good start. They have a habit of dropping in unexpectedly to see how things are growing and, needless to say, their visits keep me on my gardening toes—weeding, watering, and hoeing. Sometimes I wonder who is more pleased by the results!

In the same way, I believe it is both satisfying and mutually encouraging to follow up on those Christians who are new in the faith. They need to know that we are vitally interested in their spiritual growth and that we will rejoice with them as they successfully adjust to a different way of life. Our loving concern may be the very incentive they need to become spiritually mature Christians.

Just as a tiny seedling withstands the shock of transplanting, develops a sturdy root system, and grows into a luxurious plant, so it is gratifying to see a young Christian fulfill Psalm 92:13-14a: "Planted in the house of the LORD, they will flourish in the courts of our God. They will still yield fruit in old age."

36. CONFESSING OUR COBWEBS

Create in me a clean heart, O God, and renew a stead-fast spirit within me (Psalm 51:10).

Spring cleaning I don't mind. The interruptions are what get me down. Both ways.

I am dangling from a stepladder with a paint can in one hand and a brush in the other when the doorbell rings. Twice. Descending from the heights, I sprint down the hallway, hurdle the furniture strewn about, and kick aside the rubble barring the doorway. My caller turns out to be a lady selling cosmetics.

She seems shocked by my appearance. I can't say I blame her. It's not every day she sees hair spattered with Sea Mist Semigloss and a latex complexion to match. She backs down the steps.

I no sooner get perched up on my ladder again than the tomcat has to go out. I figure I'll just let him yowl while I paint to the corner. Oh, no, I won't! He's beginning to cringe in desperation. Down the ladder I go.

Up again, and the telephone rings. Down again. Up, down, up, down. I begin to feel like a pogo stick. As if to emphasize the point, my girl comes hopping home from school.

"Guess what, Mommy! I'm Flopsy in the play about Peter Rabbit. Teacher says we should have a costume tomorrow with ears this long and whiskers and a tail—"

"That's nice, dear." (Just who do those teachers think I am, anyway? Have they no idea what it means to make a costume in the middle of spring cleaning?)

"Look outside, Mommy. Isn't it nice out?"

As I survey the backyard from my vantage point on the stepladder, I realize it is a credit to the Almighty that He can do such a fantastic job of spring decorating despite exasperating mortals like myself encroaching on His plans. According to that great promise, however, He is never too busy to accommodate us. "All that the Father gives Me shall come to Me; and the one who comes to Me I will certainly not cast out" (John 6:37).

It feels good to pause and thank Him for His patience and love, but it also makes me aware of my own inconsiderate attitude at times. "If we confess our sins, He is faithful and righteous to forgive us our sins and to cleanse us from all unrighteousness" (1 John 1:9).

37. FALSE IMPRESSIONS

The kingdom of heaven is like a treasure hidden in the field (Matthew 13:44).

It was little Johnny's first trip to visit his relatives in the country. He was therefore quite intrigued by most of the farm animals, with the possible exception of the pigs.

"Can't say I blame you, son," his father consoled. "I think pigs have terrible manners."

"Oh, I've seen worse," replied Johnny in retrospect.

"Maybe you like the smell?" his father teased.

Johnny shrugged. "Aw, it ain't so bad I guess."

Trying to evoke a bit more response, his father exclaimed, "Pigs sure are noisy!"

"Yeah, sometimes," agreed Johnny. It was obvious something was troubling him as he shuffled along toward the house. By now his father was more than a little curious.

"Tell me, son, why don't you like pigs?"

Johnny hesitated a moment and then blurted out, "Cuz they don't have no holes in their backs for the money to go in!"

Had his father not been so persistent, he would never have guessed the real reason Johnny was acting so disgruntled. The boy had banked his hopes on false assumptions.

Sometimes we cannot understand why unbelievers are so critical of us as Christians. They do not seem to realize that we are still human, still subject to error, vulnerable to sin.

Perhaps the church has unthinkingly held up "china replicas" of the real thing—"piggy bank Christians." The unbeliever's concept of a true Christian is therefore much higher than what he actually sees in real life. Little wonder he accuses Christians of not measuring up!

Faith in Christ does not produce flawless men and women, regardless of what some people expect. Neither should we hide our weaknesses in a vain attempt to be a "perfect" witness. As Paul pointed out, we "have this treasure in earthen vessels, that the surpassing greatness of the power may be of God and not from ourselves" (2 Corinthians 4:7). Like piggy banks, we sometimes have to be broken for the benefit of skeptics, that the sum and substance of our faith can be fully appraised.

38. A DUST DETECTOR?

Be sensible, pure, workers at home (Titus 2:5a).

The phone rings. It is the neighborhood's model house-keeper calling. I can tell by the shine in her voice. She asks if I'm busy.

"Not really," I reply. "I was just vacuuming the freezer."

"Vacuuming? The freezer?" There is a slight pause. (I bet she hasn't thought of that one before.) She sounds uneasy. "You mean you actually vacuum your freezer?"

"Oh sure!" I tell her, as if I do it every day. "You'd be surprised how many corn kernels and 'twist 'ems' there are in the bottom."

"Oh, I *see*," she says, as if her bags of corn never spring leaks. I wonder if I can shatter that smug attitude by using the old shock treatment? It's worth a try, so in the course of our conversation I mention that vacuuming is certainly easier than shoveling it out.

"Shovel? Did you say *shovel?*" I can tell she is a bit horrified. She is, after all, a spotless housekeeper.

"Sure," I reply, very casually. "Why wait for all that ice to melt when you can just scrape it off the sides of the freezer and shovel it out in chunks?"

"Oh! You mean the *ice!*" She is definitely relieved, poor thing. She must have thought I was referring to dirt. (I know I'm not a perfect housekeeper, but I didn't think it was that bad!)

As Cicero said, "The comfort derived from the misery of others is slight," so I hastily apologize for teasing her along.

She is a good sport, and we laugh together about our little foibles.

Thinking later about our conversation, I begin to wonder why some people jump to conclusions over a speck of dirt. I happen to belong to that vast company of homemakers who can occasionally write their names in the dust on the dining room table. I make no apologies because I tend to think the perfectionist can scrub and wax and polish until cleaning becomes something of an obsession with her. Instead of making her home a welcome oasis, it offers about as much hospitality as an intensive-care unit. And then she wonders why her family goes somewhere else in search of relaxation!

I believe we should aim for a balance of comfort and cleanliness. A little motto I read somewhere says it very nicely: "A *real* home is clean enough to be healthy and dirty enough to be happy."

39. IN THE LIMELIGHT

Accordingly whatever you have said in the dark shall be heard in the light, and what you have whispered in the inner rooms shall be proclaimed upon the housetops (Luke 12:3).

The little guy in kindergarten informs me that he needs a big, brown grocery bag. Teacher's orders. I rummage around in the pantry while he stands there with that "ask me no questions, I'll tell you no lies" expression. Secrets are weighty stuff at age five, you see.

Soon he is galloping down the road to school with the bag billowing out behind him in the wind. I think no more about it.

On washday I find a piece of paper scrunched into the pocket of his jeans. It's an invitation to the spring concert. Featured will be an Indian powwow presented by the kindergarten class.

I ask him if he needs a costume.

"Nope." He is very smug about it. I wonder if I should take his word for it. Right up until show time I wonder.

And then, before I know it, Junior is war whooping his way across the stage, wearing the brown paper bag as a buckskin, complete with fringes. He is joined by several more young braves in war paint and chicken feathers.

Judging from the painting on their buckskins, these warriors are from more than one tribe. Let's see now—the fellow on the left is a Red Owl, the one next to him is a Piggly-Wiggly, over there we have a Safeway, and the guy with the tom-tom is a Dominion. If I'm not mistaken, I even see a few Solos and Payfairs. The grocery confederacy is well represented here tonight. It's an occasion in which the chainstore managers could take valid pride.

Little did I realize I was betraying my own loyalty when I handed Junior a brown paper bag, but my choice of supermarket was suddenly there for all to see, and it would be ridiculous to pretend otherwise.

The incident shows how relatively insignificant decisions can wind up in the spotlight of attention. "Pulling for the bad guys on TV" or "secretly" admiring the criminal may suggest to our children that we condone violence and corruption.

Circulating unfounded rumors or contributing unkind remarks may pinpoint us as a source of gossip.

Trying to conceal bad habits or boasting about shrewd business deals only invites a worse label—that of hypocrite.

Sooner or later all our decisions come to have a bearing on our Christian reputation, for "there is nothing covered up that will not be revealed, and hidden that will not be known" (Luke 12:2).

40. UNFADING BEAUTY

*Observe how the lilies of the field grow; they do not toil
nor do they spin, yet I say to you that even Solomon in
all his glory did not clothe himself like one of these*
(Matthew 6:28b-29).

The remains of a very special bouquet I received for
Mother's Day are sitting on the kitchen table. I doubt if it
would merit anything more than a curious glance from anyone but me. After all, not just anybody can appreciate three
dandelions and a stinkweed scrunched into an abandoned
baby bottle.

The dandelions have long since wilted, but the stinkweed
is bursting out in full bloom. And it's gratifying to see the
last baby's bottle pressed into active service as a flower vase
after it had already been placed on the retirement list.

Our preschooler didn't stop to consider such trivialities
as focus, line, and detail when arranging flowers. The bouquet he presented to me for Mothers' Day was noticeably
lacking in all three dimensions, but it still conveyed his mes-
sage of love. It would be cruel to refuse such a gift on the
grounds that it failed to comply with prescribed standards.

When similar tokens of love are extended toward us, how
are they received? Do we examine them with such a critical
eye that we are blind to the real values they represent? Do
we fail to show our appreciation because the gift did not cost
much in terms of dollars and cents? A perfectly arranged
bouquet delivered to my door from the florist's shop would
have probably evoked many more complimentary remarks
than a toddler's collection of weeds. My attention, however,

would be attracted to the *gift* whereas otherwise it was centered on the *giver*.

When Christ pointed to the lilies, I believe He was cautioning us about the danger of transferring our affections from the Giver (God) to the gift. In our admiration of "Solomon in all his glory," we are tempted to toil and spin in our own strength in order to be wealthy and well dressed, capable of giving expensive gifts to our friends or entertaining lavishly. Jesus, however, points us to the simple, yet profound beauty of those who are rooted in God the Father and who spontaneously reflect the deeper values that money cannot buy, "the imperishable quality of a gentle and quiet spirit, which is precious in the sight of God" (1 Peter 3:4*b*).

41. DRIVEN TO AND FRO?

I will instruct you and teach you in the way which you should go; I will counsel you with My eye upon you (Psalm 32:8).

If you see me hobbling along with my back bent in the shape of a hairpin, let me explain. Our oldest son has just received his beginner's license, and no man in this house is going to let a woman teach him how to drive. I am therefore relegated to the back seat of the two-door compact while Father assumes the position of authority by his side. Only a piece of boiled macaroni would be flexible enough to bend itself into that back seat, hence my peculiar shape.

Once inside, I have no trouble straightening out. Within half a mile we suffer such a series of close scrapes that I am stiff with fear. I unwind just long enough to give a few bits of pertinent advice, and bingo! He's shaving the bark from a telephone pole. Somehow I get the distinct feeling that a student driver is easily rattled. (I've told his father how to drive for years, and he's never paid the least bit of attention.)

I breathe a sigh of relief as we pull safely up the driveway. You've no idea how much prayer goes into backseat driving. I double up in preparation for disembarking.

On subsequent trips, I keep thinking how aptly old Nahum described the future destruction of a city by saying, "The chariots shall rage in the streets, they shall justle one against another in the broad ways" (Nahum 2:4, KJV). The accuracy of his predictions should have merited him a place of distinction, but where do we find him? In the back seat with the minor prophets! It's small consolation for those of us in similar positions, but it's better than none.

As parents, all the warnings we issue about the dangers of careless driving seem to fall upon deaf ears. Teenagers just don't seem to comprehend the seriousness of the situation, and they may even scoff at us for pointing out their bad driving habits. As those who are responsible for their present training as well as their future welfare, we need not apologize for what appears to be backseat driving.

Someday the advice we have given may spare them from a serious accident, and they will realize that what we have said all along was true.

In the meantime, "some trust in chariots, and some in horses; but we will remember the name of the LORD our God" (Psalm 20:7, KJV). I can just hear all the mothers of student drivers as they straighten up and shout, "Amen!"

42. FROM RAGS TO RICHES

For all of us have become like one who is unclean, and all our righteous deeds are like a filthy garment (Isaiah 64:6).

It's spring again, and time to take the winter's accumulation of junk to the nuisance ground. The day we went, the garbage pickers were having a ball. I think I'll join the union. Fellows were swapping old tires for tree limbs and sawhorses for sealers. The white elephants were being recycled before they even hit the ground.

When I was young, the nuisance ground was regarded by farmers as their main source of scrap iron. Instead of being looked upon with disdain, it provided a practical illustration of give and take. You donated what you couldn't use and took what you could. Consequently, many rebuilt pieces of machinery could have been used as symbols of community enterprise.

The spirit of ingenuity rubbed off on the boys in particular. One little fellow observed his older brothers dragging home spare bicycle parts from the garbage dump. Trying to imitate their behavior, he rounded up some discarded metal and announced proudly, "Here I come with a piece of nuisance!" To his way of thinking, it was the ultimate achievement.

Somehow I think God feels a little like that when He salvages some of the wrecks of humanity. On the surface, mankind must appear to Him as little more than a heap of refuse. Imagine, then, a piece of garbage standing up of its own accord and declaring itself fit for service! Even from the human standpoint the idea appears ridiculous. And yet, with supreme love and insight God overlooks such futile claims of self-sufficiency and gently points to our condition. What we see there in comparison to God's holiness is not a pretty picture, but one of filth, decay, and corruption.

Instead of turning up His nose, God lifts us up by His grace and makes us fit for His Kingdom. Every believer was once "a piece of nuisance," condemned because of the sinful condition of human nature. Through faith in Christ he has been resurrected to the abundant life. "Therefore if any man is in Christ, he is a new creature; the old things passed away; behold, new things have come" (2 Corinthians 5:17).

43. STIFF NECKS AND DIRTY

All the ways of a man are clean in his own sight, but the Lord weighs the motives (Proverbs 16:2).

I tell our boy to go and wash his face. Just as I expected, he retorts indignantly, "My face *is* clean!"

I grab him by the ear for a closer examination. "Your face may be clean, but there's a high-water mark along your jawbone."

"Aw, that's cuz there was lots of flooding this spring, Mom. Be glad the water only came up that far."

"You'd never drown as long as there was a bar of soap in it, that's for sure! Now go and wash your face."

"But you said my face was clean."

"All right, then, go and wash your neck."

He takes a fast peek in the mirror. "That's not dirt. That's my beard. It's just starting to grow."

"And since when do three whiskers cast that much of a shadow?"

"I dunno. I suppose it depends where the sun is."

"Look, fella, it's been dark for two hours. Now go and wash your neck before you go to bed!"

"Do I have to?"

"Yes! You have to!" To the side I mutter, "Talk about a stiff-necked people!"

"What was that you said about my neck?"

"I may threaten to wring it if you don't wash it soon!"

"Oh, all right, Mom! If it means that much to you, I'll go and do it." And he shuffles off to the bathroom.

It's surprising how many of us think we are just doing

God a favor by leading a "clean" life. We fail to see that the moral guidelines God sets out are for our own benefit, and so we resist certain principles because we consider them little more than the whims of an almighty dictator.

Every so often God has to "grab us by the ear" and show us our reflection in the Bible. We see there that when the children of Israel abandoned God's ways, they quickly lost their sense of dignity and worth, sinking to the level of the heathen nations around them in terms of immorality and false worship.

Looking at Christianity today, we need to pray with Moses, "Go among us; for [we are] . . . a stiffnecked people; and pardon our iniquity and our sin, and take us for thine inheritance" (Exodus 34:9, KJV).

44. ODOR ODDITIES

For we are a fragrance of Christ to God among those who are being saved and among those who are perishing (2 Corinthians 2:15).

Every so often you get a whiff of something that triggers off a whole chain of reminiscences. I walked into the bathroom a few minutes ago and the lingering traces of air freshner reminded me of Lifebuoy soap—*the* Lifebuoy soap, the original orange-pink bar with the hexagon corners that graced the old washstand in farm kitchens. Everybody who crossed paths with a bar of Lifebuoy came away feeling cleaner, and smelling it, too. At one point it seemed the entire rural population was a walking billboard. Suddenly the soap tycoons switched perfumes, and we had to pay for more sophisticated but less effective forms of advertising.

Hair tonic seemed to hold its own a bit longer, despite the fact that it smelled like perfumed chicken fat, rancid at that. When the spring winds beckoned, many a young man with hair slicked down shiny went courting a girl friend who sported a frizzy home permanent, traces of which, when exposed to warm sunshine, faintly resembled a skunk.

Speaking of spring, about the time the lilacs began to bloom out yonder, someone would inadvertently drown out their fragrance by disinfecting the outhouse with creosote. Even though the horseflies made fewer reconnaissance flights from beyond the corral, creosote never did compensate for lilacs in springtime.

What I find peculiar is that people seem to interpret odors differently. What is perfumy to one person is pungent to another. Friend hubby detests brushing against geranium leaves, while I think their scent is rather invigorating. And while I go around pinching tomato vines because they speak to me of "beefsteak cologne," friend hubby walks circumspectly around the plant to avoid contagion.

The apostle Paul reminds us that, as believers, we represent the "sweet savor" of Christ. Not everyone, however, will interpret our behavior as "sweet" (and sometime for valid reasons!), nor will they "savor" our presence if it means embarrassment to them in an uncomfortable situation.

We should remember that rare perfumes have subtle appeal, and a dab behind each ear is about all that is required. Instead of gently attracting people toward Christ, however, some Christians feel they must "come on strong." Overwhelmed by such a bold confrontation with the gospel, unbelievers may actually find it repulsive.

Just as we use perfume with discretion, so we must use discernment in approaching people about salvation. It is reassuring to know that even so humble an effort as a life daily committed to Christ leaves lingering traces of testimony wherever we go, and "manifests through us the sweet aroma of the knowledge of Him in every place" (2 Corinthians 2:14*b*).

45. CURATIVE POWER

*When he saw him, he felt compassion, and came to him,
and bandaged up his wounds, pouring oil and wine on
them* (Luke 10:33b-34a).

Listening to others discuss various remedies for their aches
and pains, I've concluded that we must either be particularly healthy in this family or else extremely long-suffering.

About all my medicine chest contains is a few bandages,
some cough syrup, and a can of carbolic salve, the latter a
carry-over from the good old days. It used to come in a
round can ornately painted in red and gold. "Good for man
or beast" was the slogan on top. Farmers since time im-
memorial have used it to patch up that part of a low-slung
cow which invariably got caught in the fence when she decided to trespass to greener pastures.

I used to watch my mother doctoring up various domestic
animals. Being next in line as the self-appointed vet in the
family, I would spirit the can of carbolic salve out to the
pigpen at a very young age in an attempt to soothe any
scratches inflicted by the barbed wire fence. The pigs were
always very uncooperative.

The old collie dog, on the other hand, was very flattered
by my attention. Detecting some imaginary wound or other,
I would grease him up at length, whereupon he would
promptly begin to lick it all off.

Carbolic salve must not be fatal. That dog probably ate
pounds of it in the course of his life and still lived to a ripe
old age.

I suppose, like all patent medicine, it never did him a great deal of harm.

But then, it never did him any good either.

While we are encouraged to follow the example set by the good Samaritan in ministering to the physically or spiritually wounded, we must recognize that there is a limit to what we can do for some people. Or perhaps I should say there is *no* limit!

You have probably had the experience of greeting someone with "How are you today?" only to have her take it literally. Jumping at the opportunity to engage in her favorite pastime, she promptly gives you a complete and total rundown of all current ailments, plus a lengthy account of her past medical history. Regardless of what we may try to do or say in terms of easing the suffering of such hypochondriacs, they continue to *"enjoy* poor health."

Then there are the spiritual hypochondriacs, like the fellow who seems either unwilling or unable to forgive and forget past wounds. He never really allows his "sore spots" to heal, but keeps picking away at the scab, encouraging even more scar tissue. Self-conscious of his spiritual disfigurement, he eventually withdraws into the background, despite the sincere efforts of concerned Christians to be of help.

I may sound hardhearted, but I refuse to sympathize with such individuals, not because it will do any harm, but because it so seldom does any good. Easing the suffering is not a patent remedy for self-pity. The afflicted person must seek a cure from the One who "heals the brokenhearted, and binds up their wounds" (Psalm 147:3).

46. FRESH BEGINNINGS

Wash me thoroughly from my iniquity, and cleanse me from my sin (Psalm 51:2).

My old wringer washer is gone. As they toted it up the stairs and out into oblivion, I felt as if I were parting from an old friend. It wasn't perfect—friends never claim to be—but somehow I hadn't noticed until now. Oh, there were a couple of casters missing, the hose was wired on and patched with friction tape, the pump had gone on strike, and the wringer worked only in reverse. But those faults were only minor details. It had washed the family's clothes since day one, a tried and true companion who shared my Monday-morning blues.

That old battle-scarred veteran of a bygone era has now been replaced, the age of automation having crept across my basement and cornered me into buying an automatic washer. It has, by comparison, a very introverted personality. Beneath its cold white exterior there lurks any number of mysterious schemes. It even mumbles to itself, some kind of incomprehensible jargon nobody can interpret.

I was always on speaking terms with the old wringer washer. If it chugged or groaned or squawked, I instinctively ran to its assistance. An automatic washer is extremely independent. I offend it if I even so much as open the lid. Everything stops short, and I'm made to feel like an intruder, no matter how well meaning my intentions.

I sometimes wonder if that's how we react to God. We think we can carry on independently behind His back, our life-style selfishly programmed to suit our own current needs.

Now and then God in His wisdom attempts to reschedule our man-made schemes, but our conscience simply "shuts down" in His presence, and we continue on with our own prearranged plans.

Although fully automatic, a washer cannot function without electricity and water, and neither can we fulfill the intended purpose for our lives apart from God's power and presence. We may have great potential, but until we acknowledge God as our ultimate source of strength, all our "programming" is but a ridiculous effort to prove our own self-sufficiency.

As fiercely independent as we have become in this age of automation, it is a humbling experience to return to the old "scrub-board of repentance" and there claim total reliance upon God. King David recognized the stains of rebellion in his soul, and getting down on his knees, he wrung his heart out in confession as he sought God's promised forgiveness. "Purify me with hyssop, and I shall be clean; wash me, and I shall be whiter than snow" (Psalm 51:7).

47. DEAD MICE IN OUR DISHES

But you, are you seeking great things for yourself? Do not seek them (Jeremiah 45:5a).

I am raising a very citified tomcat. After feeding him all winter, he was still as gaunt as a one-by-six board.

Come spring, I told him in no uncertain terms to get out and catch a mouse. I even made him a toy so he would recognize his prey, but it was easier to sit on the step and soak up the sunshine than to prowl around in search of rodents.

All right then. I would put him out at night so he wouldn't be tempted to sleep in the sun.

I'm afraid he yielded to other temptations. He came home in the morning, starved to death.

I hinted very strongly that a tomcat who couldn't catch a mouse wasn't worth his own hide.

Yesterday he fooled me. He came home with a mouse, right at suppertime. Smuggled it into the kitchen and laid it in his dish.

Even from my vantage point atop the kitchen stool I could tell something was amiss. This mouse was not a recent kill. In fact, the tomcat never even offered to eat it. He just wanted it there as a status symbol.

Try and get it away from him, though. That was another story.

Like the tomcat, it's ironic how fiercely we defend the things we haven't earned, can't afford, and seldom use. But we hang on anyway, playing the game of "let's pretend" with our status symbols.

Perhaps the "dead mouse in your dish" is that second car in the garage or that expensive set of china in your cupboard or that stylish new dress in your closet. You have felt just a twinge of guilt paying so much money for something you so seldom use, but you enjoy it. That's the main thing. Or is it?

Do you not also feel just a wee bit of satisfaction knowing that you have managed to get on equal footing with the neighbors? Or maybe even one step *ahead* of them?

Social pressure is a powerful force in today's society, and even Christians can be sidetracked into believing that it is important to conform in material ways in order to make a good impression. Before long, however, we begin equating God's blessings in terms of material prosperity. Even though common sense tells us it is wiser to "let go" of certain possessions, it becomes a real struggle to do so. Was this item not one of God's favors bestowed upon me? Why then should it be revoked so suddenly? How will I explain it to the neighbors? They'll conclude I'm going downhill financially. Isn't that a disgrace for a Christian?

Our human response is to hang on and hope. Spiritually, however, we should be prepared to say with Job: "The LORD gave and the LORD has taken away. Blessed be the name of the LORD" (Job 1:21*b*).

48. JUST KNOCK

Behold, I stand at the door and knock; if any one hears My voice and opens the door, I will come in to him, and will dine with him, and he with Me (Revelation 3:20).

It happens all the time. Minutes after the alarm goes off in the morning, the doorbell rings. I shuffle down the hall in my housecoat to find an innocent-looking cherub standing on the back step. "Can Susie come out to play?"

"Susie is still sleeping."

"OK, I'll come back later." She makes one lap around the house. The doorbell rings again. "Is Susie up yet?"

Two laps around the house. "Has Susie had breakfast yet?"

Three laps. "Mrs. Barkman, are you mad at me?"

"Not exactly. Why?"

"Cuz you're foaming at the mouth. My mommy says if Rover foams at the mouth, he's going crazy, and we have to get rid of him."

"Tell your mother I'm just trying to brush my teeth."

"I can't. She's still sleeping."

It puzzles me how kids two feet tall can scale the brick molding in order to reach the doorbell, yet they do it all the time. My doorbell even has the peanut butter and jelly fingerprints to prove it. My talkative little intruders seem to take Matthew 7:7 literally: "Ask, and it shall be given to you; seek, and you shall find; knock, and it shall be opened to you." Or as my persistent little friend remarked, "Ya gotta knock cuz God doesn't have a doorbell. Right, Mrs. Barkman?"

How mankind would take unfair advantage of God's hospitality if we could just ring the doorbell of heaven and the gates would swing wide to accommodate us! Why, the mansions would be jammed to capacity!

God has different plans, however. Instead of allowing heaven to become a "free for all," God stipulates that it is reserved for "whosoever will." Just as our home is a refuge for family and friends and not a public "drop-in center," so access to heaven is secured by personal faith in Christ, who said, "I am the door; if anyone enters through Me, he shall be saved" (John 10:9).

How secure it feels to be a child of God, to know that at any time of the day or night we have a standing invitation to heaven. Remember, though, you have to knock, "cuz God doesn't have a doorbell!"

49. THE FLUSH FLOOD

Then the flood came upon the earth for forty days; and the water increased and lifted up the ark, so that it rose above the earth (Genesis 7:17).

Our youngest son trailed along behind me when I went to the neighbor's for coffee yesterday. We were no sooner there than he informed me he had to use the bathroom. I heard the toilet flush and half expected to see him come hobbling down the hall with his pants down around his ankles.

Several minutes went by. *Good,* I thought, *he's finally learning to pull up his jeans in the privacy of the bathroom.*

When several more minutes had elapsed, I went to investigate. Apparently the toilet had failed to flush properly, and he was standing there, fascinated by the water as it swirled treacherously close to the rim of the bowl. Horrified that the premises would soon be inundated, I yelled for my hostess to come to the rescue.

"Oh, never mind that!" she called back from the kitchen. "Does it all the time. Never runs over, though."

Had I been in her shoes, I'd have tried any number of things—grabbed the toilet plunger, turned off the water supply, phoned the plumber. But no, she sauntered down the hall and stood in the doorway sipping her coffee, calmly waiting for the waters to recede.

Now that, I thought, *is faith—akin to the quality of Noah's.*

It's comparatively easy to say we believe in the overall power of God when things are flowing along normally—no plugged traps or storm sewer backups. But when circumstances threaten to overwhelm us, we suddenly question God's wisdom in allowing such near catastrophes. Alarmed and somewhat panic-stricken, we feel our frail little ark of faith begin to tremble and shake; then we humbly admit that it is not the stout seagoing vessel we had imagined it to be.

I am sure Noah also had his moments of doubt as the "waters increased," but there was little he could do to escape from the situation. So he simply trusted God all the more as that big, old ark creaked and heaved along with its strange cargo, the floodwaters testing it at every point.

Likewise, it is only as we accept God's will and rest completely in Him that we are "lifted above the earth"—given the strength to overcome even the most trying conditions. "Therefore we will not fear, though the earth should change, and though the mountains slip into the heart of the sea; though its waters roar and foam" (Psalm 46:2-3a).

50. WHAT WILL WE LEAVE BEHIND?

So teach us to number our days, that we may present to Thee a heart of wisdom (Psalm 90:12).

A neighbor says she dreads the day when she will depart for the great beyond because her relatives will discover what messy closets she left behind.

As for me, I can just imagine the things they'll say about my freezers. What I regard as the potential of some great gastronomical delight is just so much frozen bulk to people of lesser imagination.

My theory is simple: If it's edible, freeze it. I can worry about recipes later. It so happens that I end up with a freezer full of food in various stages of preparedness. Only a genius could guess what each container holds. You see, I have an excellent memory, theoretically speaking, and as a result I don't bother to label half the packages. It's the power of recall that fouls me up. I forget what I have frozen.

Today I decided to delve into the mystery. I defrosted the freezer and brought all these cartons upstairs to thaw.

I shall be baking until midnight. There is apple mush, grape pulp, banana mash, and apricot puree, to name a few. I drag out all my related recipes, grease my pans, and set to work.

The first cake off the assembly line is an applesauce loaf. Now, Dr. Seuss had his fun telling kids about *Green Eggs and Ham.* For some strange reason, the soda must have reacted adversely with the bright pink applesauce I used, so tonight dessert will be green cake and jam.

It's the kind of unique legacy for which mothers are long remembered, but which we would much rather forget.

We leave another legacy behind, apart from that vast treasure store of memories that is every child's natural inheritance. As a mother I hope I am able to convey in some small way the benefits of a life dedicated to God.

In a world that seems to snatch and claw for material gain, I hope my children have seen in me a higher motive for making money than simply for selfish reasons. I hope, too, that they have sensed contentment in my role as wife and mother, that I have acted worthy of that sacred calling and conducted myself accordingly.

I hope they have seen the pleasure to be found in the practical aspects of living—the challenge of baking bread, making quilts, or canning. I hope, too, that they realize the savings involved were part of my stewardship and although the sense of achievement I enjoyed was only a side benefit, it was very rewarding all the same.

And, regardless of the circumstances that face them, I hope my life will be remembered as a practical illustration of Hebrews 13:5, "Let your way of life be free from the love of money, being content with what you have; for He Himself has said, 'I WILL NEVER DESERT YOU, NOR WILL I EVER FORSAKE YOU.'"

51. MIXED FEELINGS

For we have become partakers of Christ, if we hold fast the beginning of our assurance firm until the end (Hebrews 3:14).

There are two months in the school year that I still recall quite vividly. They are September and June; the beginning and the end.

Compared to the agony of September, June was pure ecstacy. Oh, it had its drawbacks like boring review lessons and year-end examinations, but it also had its ball games, its track and field day, its school picnic, and its class outing.

Nowadays they call them "field trips." Way back then we referred to them as "nature hikes." They are not to be confused with those trips we made out yonder just so we could escape the stifling atmosphere of the classroom. Those were nature hikes of a different sort. (We made plenty of those, too.)

No, the nature hikes I remember were always made in June. We were to gather all the information we could about our natural surroundings and then compile a class report on environment.

It was the one occasion of the year in which country kids came into their own. Why, we discovered we actually knew more than our city-bred schoolteacher! It was a heady experience.

Feeling a little guilty for undermining her confidence like that, we compensated with bouquets of lilacs and wild roses. Her desk banked with floral arrangements, she must have felt like a movie star on opening night, except for the bugs, bees, and worms infesting her classroom.

Come June 30th, we were torn both ways. Ahead of us stretched two glorious months of freedom, but we also had to say good-bye to the teacher. Amid an emotional exchange of gifts and cramped speeches, it was difficult to "discern between the shouts of joy and the noise of weeping" (from Ezra 3:13). No reflection on the teacher, mind you, but the shouts of joy were always a bit louder, as I recall.

There are many experiences of life in which we find ourselves torn both ways. Leaving an old familiar neighborhood for a home in another city has its share of poignant memories coupled with the excitement of adventure.

Saying good-bye to your child as he begins his first day of school evokes both satisfaction and uncertainty. You are glad he has reached this milestone, but you wonder how well he will adjust to this new experience.

Joy and sorrow both stir within you as you pay your last respects to a loved one who suffered much and has now gone home to be with the Lord. You know he is beyond the reach of pain, but you also experience the very real loss that comes with the death of someone dear.

It is comforting to know that in the Christian walk we have One who is with us through all of life's emotional turmoils. When overcome by sorrow, we can claim His promise that "weeping may last for the night, but a shout of joy comes in the morning" (Psalm 30:5b).

52. FOWL PRIDE

You do not know what your life will be like tomorrow
(James 4:14*a*).

The smaller kids asked why we were waiting until after
dark to catch the chickens.

"Because that's when they're nice and quiet. They're just
going to sleep."

"But you shouldn't catch them then!" they protested.
"They might just be saying their prayers!"

If I were as close to my reward as those chickens, I'd be
saying my prayers too! As we descended upon the chicken
house we could hear occasional muffled crowing. The
"amens" perhaps?

The chickens offered very little resistance as we stuffed
them into their crates. (Actually, all I did was to sit on the
board so they couldn't jump out again. My friend was doing
the catching.)

At one point I seemed to be sitting on my board rather
longer than usual. I timidly inquired as to the delay. It so
happened that my friend was groping around the dark
chicken coop in search of a particular pair of drumsticks.
She didn't elaborate and the explanation was rather stifled,
but it was better than none. After what seemed hours, she
emerged triumphant. Tipping a grotesque assortment of
feathers right side up, she declared, "This is the one I intend
to keep."

I can't say I blame her. He flapped his wings a couple of
times to restore his dignity, and I realized at once that I had

never laid eyes upon such a magnificent specimen of rooster-hood.

Slowly and thoughtfully he walked between the crates, peering at his less fortunate brothers with haughty disdain. His ego thus properly inflated, he stuck out his chest, crowed mightily, and promptly retired for the night.

If he had only known how close his call had been—

It is enjoyable to plan for the future, to set certain goals, and then work toward them. It is even more thrilling to achieve those goals. But what is our reaction to "success"? Do we turn right around and scorn the fellow who has been less fortunate?

I have seen people glowing with pride at their own accomplishments and at the same time condemning their fellow-men as "failures."

It is not for us to know why God allows some people to have "all the breaks" while others seem to be hindered time and again in whatever they attempt. We do know that sooner or later our turn will come, one way or another.

In the meantime, all our boastings are of no significance. "You ought to say, 'If the Lord wills, we shall live and also do this or that' " (James 4:15).

Nothing more. Nothing less.

53. EASING THE TENSION

Oh spare me, that I may recover strength, before I go hence, and be no more (Psalm 39:13, KJV).

My neighbor recently found himself at the top of an extension ladder painting a three-story house. He had managed relatively well until the last day when a strong wind came up rather suddenly.

He was painting the trim around the very top window when he realized his arm had begun to shrink. Well, not exactly, but the window was moving farther away.

It dawned upon him that his ladder had begun to slide—sideways. The agony would have been less severe had he gone with a bang. But no, he claims he had all the time in the world to consider his alternatives but too little time in which to decide.

He was acutely aware that if he spilled his green paint on the neighboring house he'd have another job lined up whether he liked it or not. At this point the idea was not exactly appealing. He made a grab for the eave, but missed.

Looking down, he realized he would have a choice of landings—the concrete driveway, the rosebushes, or astride the picket fence. If need be, he would opt for the rosebushes, thorns and all.

He was prepared for the inevitable when the ladder caught on the telephone wire leading into the house. The wire stretched, easing the ladder downward, and our painter stepped off with all the aplomb of a high-wire aerialist. He hadn't spilled a drop of paint, but the day took on a different color just the same.

As we go along from day to day, there is a real tendency to take life for granted. Then, through a series of circumstances, God changes our outlook. Perhaps we find ourselves teetering on the ladder of success or walking the tightrope of imminent financial failure. Perhaps heart disease threatens our life, or our marriage partners warn us of their intention to walk out of the relationship.

At such critical points, the choices before us may not seem pleasant. Whichever way we fall, it appears we will be subjected to pain and humiliation.

Then God in His goodness undertakes for us in our helpless condition and eases us through the situation as only He can do.

Reflecting back upon the experience, we see that God has given us a new appreciation for life. "Now unto him that is able to keep you from falling, and to present you faultless before the presence of his glory with exceeding joy, to the only wise God our Saviour, be glory and majesty, dominion and power, both now and ever" (Jude 24-25, KJV).

54.   THE NEAT STREAK

Let us therefore draw near with confidence to the throne of grace, that we may receive mercy and may find grace to help in time of need (Hebrews 4:16).

We are acutely conscious that the teenager is in the midst of yet another adolescent phase. After using the expression "neat" to describe everything from weird hairdos to outlandish cars, the real meaning of the word has actually sunk home. He has begun to pick up after himself.

Where once upon a time his bedroom was a conglomerate of corporate affairs, it is now singularly tidy. No more dirty socks draped over the mirror, no jeans hanging from the bedpost, no wood shavings on the floor. The leatherwork tools are assembled in one box, the sports equipment is stacked in the closet, and the tape deck is even dusted. And miracles happen! The bed is even made.

Nor is he content to restrain his efforts to his own room. I am frequently being reminded that my dishes are not done, the newspapers are scattered, and the lawn needs mowing.

When he came home from school the other day and discovered a muddy footprint on the kitchen floor, he declared, "This place is a mess!"

Instead of defending my oversight, I decided to put him to the test. "Yes, I know the floor's mussy, but somehow or other I haven't had time to wash it."

Whereupon he grabbed a paper towel, wiped up the mud, and asked "Is there anything else I could do to help?" His willingness to assist instead of complain came as a shock. Could it be he has actually grown up?

I think we have all experienced the feelings of discouragement which come when we attempt to fulfill some responsibility and even our best efforts are criticized by those who are either unwilling or unable to help. Many church organizations are undermined by this attitude among the members, and potential workers are fearful of becoming involved.

What makes this critical spirit so prevalent among believers? Is it ignorance or immaturity? I suggest it is a little of both.

Many people looking in on a situation cannot fathom the complexity of the program. It is so easy to see something strictly from one viewpoint—our own. But those actively involved have different priorities, and look at the situation differently, and so the friction begins.

On the other hand, there are those who do not sense the *need* for supporting a given program. They have been so dependent on others that they have not grown to the point where they see it is their turn to assist instead of just criticizing.

It would probably be a real shock if some of us could muster up sufficient grace to help instead of hinder. "Therefore, strengthen the hands that are weak and the knees that are feeble" (Hebrews 12:12).

55. NEVER WASTING, NEVER WANTING

And when they were filled, He said to His disciples, "Gather up the leftover fragments that nothing may be lost" (John 6:12).

I don't really avoid unpleasant tasks, like cleaning out the refrigerator. I just never get around to doing them. What happened recently was a natural consequence, I suppose.

I had made this huge pot of soup, you see. Now everybody knows that homemade soup tastes better if it's warmed over, so I squeezed it into the refrigerator overnight in anticipation of a feast the following day. In this house, such great expectations seldom come to pass.

Around midnight somebody must have come along to raid the fridge and completely overlooked the law of leftovers. Such a law should be prominently posted in every kitchen of the nation. It reads as follows: "The contents of any given refrigerator are delicately balanced, and one must exercise extreme caution so as not to disturb the equilibrium thereof."

I'm afraid that whoever raided my refrigerator had a complete disregard for such law and order. Worse yet, the culprit had long since disappeared when I first noticed the disaster: a puddle of soup was forming on the kitchen floor. It was slowly seeping out from the bottom of the refrigerator.

I opened the door. Horrors! There was soup in the salmon, soup in the lemon pie, soup among the onions; soup was everywhere. As far as the eye could see, nothing but soup. The only thing not soaked in soup was the pot itself. It was bone dry.

116

There was nothing for me to do but clean up the whole sordid mess. As I sopped up the last traces, washed out the refrigerator, and stood back to admire my handiwork, I felt I could better identify with Paul when he humbly confessed, "I have nothing to glory of: for necessity is laid upon me" (1 Corinthians 9:16, KJV). I'm sure that's the secret behind a great many achievements.

Unless there is a real urgency about it, work always seems to "get put and not done." I wonder just how much any of us would achieve if left to accomplish things in our own good time. Looking behind some of my own so-called achievements, I have to admit that they came about as a result of necessity, not as a result of personal initiative. I learned to bake in order to balance the budget. I learned to sew in order to have a comfortable fit in clothing. I began writing because a certain creative streak demanded an outlet. Nevertheless, all of these accomplishments that seemed to be forced upon me initially have since produced many satisfying experiences.

The same could be said of our spiritual growth. As we are forced into new circumstances where we are expected to study the Bible, we grow far more rapidly in the Word than when we are left on our own initiative. Like Paul, however, we dare not take the honor for ourselves but acknowledge God's leading in our lives and His sovereign will that "nothing be lost " that could be used for His glory.

56. YOURS FOR THE PICKING

All discipline for the moment seems not to be joyful, but sorrowful; yet to those who have been trained by it, afterwards it yields the peaceful fruit of righteousness (Hebrews 12:11).

The remnant of the vanishing breed known as berry pickers has enjoyed an unusually good summer. Afraid of being conscripted as they round up their syrup pails and head for the bush, I deliberately maintain an attitude of indifference.

Nobody in the world faces more formidable obstacles for so little reward—mosquitoes, black flies, ant hills, barbed wire fences, mad bulls, irate farmers, grand canyons, and muskegs, to name but a few. Add to this the risk of getting lost, compounded by sunstroke or pneumonia, and you have a faint idea of what berry picking is all about. (I never mentioned the nervous exhaustion suffered on the way home. It stems from the noise of three dried berries rattling around in the bottom of the pail.)

To my knowledge, it has never been fully ascertained whether wild fruit falls in the category of public domain, so the haunting question of ownership plagues the conscience with every handful of berries. "What if the owner of these trees catches me on his property and hauls me off to court on a charge of grand larceny?" or "what if he waives court procedures and demands all my berries here and now as the penalty for trespassing?" These and other equally disturbing thoughts pester the imagination. It is enough to thwart the incentive of all but the most inveterate berry pickers.

My skeptical attitude does not daunt them in the least,

however. Oh, the joy they experience when they return home after a successful day in the berry patch! Smug "I told you so" grins mirror their sense of satisfaction, and pails heaped high with berries are tangible evidence of the significant truth—perseverance does indeed "yield the peaceful fruit of righteousness to them who are exercised by it."

Their courageous example also illustrates another valuable lesson. The fruit of the Spirit (Galatians 5:22) is not plucked at leisure, but prayerfully sought by those who are willing to sacrifice in obedience to God's will. At times we may feel that our efforts in the "berry patch" of Christian living are not worth the results, but Paul reminds us in Galatians 6:8-9, "One who sows to the Spirit shall from the Spirit reap eternal life. And let us not lose heart in doing good, for in *due time* we shall reap if we do not grow weary" (italics added).

57. "CAN YOU JUST IMAGINE!"

Because to every purpose there is time and judgment, therefore the misery of man is great upon him (Ecclesiastes 8:6, KJV).

I was driving home from a dental appointment last week when what should I spy with my one thawed eye than one of the local policemen. He stuck his head in the car window.

"Where you been, ma'am?"

"At the dentisht's."

"Is that so? Any proof?"

"Jusht a frozshen jaw."

"That account for the thick tongue, too?"

"Yesh, shir, it doesh."

"This your car?"

"No, shir, it'sh borrowed."

"Can I see the registration?"

I squinted down the steering column with my one good eye. All I could see was an elastic band where the registration papers should have been.

"What about a driver's license?"

"Yesh, shir, it'sh right in my pursh—shomewhere."

"You always shake like that?"

"No, shir, jusht when I come from the dentisht's."

"You afraid of dentists?"

"Yesh, shir, I am!"

"Ever had a driving offense?"

"No, shir; I'm afraid of polischmen, too."

"Just doing a routine check, ma'am. No need to be afraid."

The family was out to greet me as I staggered up the walk.

"Wow! Mom, what did the dentist do to you?"

"Frozsh my jaw." I was drooling down my chin again.

"Did he pull all your teeth at once?"

"No, but I got pulled in by the police."

"What *for?*"

"Nothing."

"Then how come you look scared stiff?"

Have you every tried to explain what *could* have happened to a bunch of kids just itching to expand the story? To let them tell it, their mother is about to be hauled off to the county jail to serve a term for car theft, after pleading guilty to the lesser charge of drunken driving. Kids have no mercy whatever.

Gossip has even less.

While I believe there is a need for personal sharing of one another's burdens within the fellowship of believers, I would caution the wife who brings her husband's faults out into the limelight of public opinion, or the mother who lists her teenager's problems in detail. Such a breach of confidence can very often create far deeper problems.

"Talk therapy" has its place, but not where there is a risk that someone listening might break the confidence placed in him. Christian or not, it is difficult for most people to refrain from repeating what they have heard, and quite a number even take the liberty of adding something to it! Whatever we do, wherever we go, however it happens, gossip seems to bring misery and fear to the human heart. Therefore, "keep your tongue from evil, and your lips from speaking deceit" (Psalm 34:13).

58. GONE FISHING

Simon Peter said to them, "I am going fishing." They said to him, "We will also come with you" (John 21: 3a).

Like the disciples of old, the men in this family look upon fishing as an ideal excuse to get away from it all. Somehow I always get the raw end of the deal.

Now, cleaning fish is not a trick I have mastered as yet, probably because the opportunities to practice are so few and far between. Occasionally somebody lands a sucker. Now, no self-respecting fisherman's wife is going to be caught dead in one of those gory fish-cleaning stations with so humble a specimen of fishhood as a sucker. Rather than suffer the humiliation, I sneak behind the biggest clump of trees I can find, get down on my knees, and start cleaning the brute. Somehow the fish never want to cooperate. Did you ever notice that they can be dead for hours and still show no signs of rigor mortis?

When at last I emerge from the bushes, my fingers are swaddled in Band Aids, I am doused with mosquito repellent from head to toe, and all I have to show for my efforts are a couple of ragged fillets huddled in the far corner of the frying pan. To a certain young fisherman, however, those fillets are as precious as any trophy specimen mounted for display in a master angler's rec room.

As our son hovers about the stove watching the pieces sizzle to a golden brown, the pride and satisfaction in his beaming face convince me that even so detestable a task as cleaning fish can be worthwhile.

Likewise, there are some responsibilities in life that are looked upon as "fish-cleaning duties"—those unpleasant tasks which give little or no satisfaction in terms of achievement. There are, however, other compensations.

The ward aide emptying bedpans feels a certain reward in seeing the sincere gratitude expressed by a paralyzed patient. Or the fellow collecting garbage is encouraged to see it neatly bagged or bundled by thoughtful people along his route. Or the mother washing diapers (forever, so it seems) is repaid by the smile that spreads across her baby's face.

Though the call to be "fishers of men" appears on the surface to be a noble excuse to "get away from it all," it may, in reality, involve the very menial task of "cleaning the catch." If we watch for them, there are fringe benefits to be derived from those jobs we don't especially enjoy doing.

59. HOMESPUN TREASURES

And he said, "What have they seen in your house?"
(2 Kings 20:15a).

It never fails. When the living room resembles the back entrance to a printing press and I'm ready to explode about all the newspapers lying around, some fellow invites himself in and starts explaining the latest fire insurance policy. Or when the basement is so cluttered I'm afraid of spraining my ankle in the debris, the meter reader comes. He has to trace the cold-water pipe in order to find the gauge.

And every time the kitchen looks like the aftermath of hurricane Gourmet, some model housekeeper comes canvassing for charity. Her vacant stare is probably from shock.

Last week there were several pairs of pantyhose festooning the bathroom plus a pair of unmentionables draped over the shower faucet. Who should knock on the door but the plumber? It seems he had forgotten to install a flange around one of the pipes, and since he was in the neighborhood anyway, why not drop in? He barged right past me and straight down the hall to the bathroom before I could warn him.

But the real disaster area is at the back door. I may as well concede right here and now that I'll never be admitted to the annals of "Good Housekeeping." I would fail the entrance exam.

I have struggled for twenty years trying to convince myself that it is not really important what visitors *see* in my home, but how they are made to *feel*. Unfortunately, social pressure would have us believe otherwise.

We are bombarded on every side by advertisements reminding us that any homemaker worth her apron has a gleaming stove, sparkling windows, shining floors, and a bathroom smelling of lilacs.

I have, on occasion, managed to achieve one or another of these goals, but seldom simultaneously with any other. And never, ever, when company drops in unexpectedly.

To my knowledge, however, friends have never commented about my stove, other than to remark about how good the fresh bread smells. And they seem willing enough to overlook the smudges on my windows and floors, occasionally even adding a few of their own. When it comes to the bathroom, only a dreamer expects lilacs in January.

In short, I think it is safe to assume that guests usually know what they are looking for, regardless of the condition in which they find our house. I pray that "there is nothing among my treasures that I have not shown them" in terms of fun and Christian fellowship (2 Kings 20:15c).

60. A EULOGY

Let me die the death of the upright, and let my end be like his (Numbers 23:10*b*).

My tomcat is no more.

For some unknown reason, the intricacies of his digestive system went berserk, and he no longer made it to his litter box with any degree of predictability. Attached as I was to the old villain, I detested cleaning up after him. All the same, I felt he deserved a second chance, so I managed to obtain a reprieve for him after his first offense.

Just when I thought I had him rehabilitated, he let me down.

I miss his furry old hide rubbing against my legs when I make supper. He never lacked ideas when it came to the menu, that was certain.

He was so adept at conversational meowing that he could keep up a running commentary on any current topic while sitting on his lofty perch atop my kitchen stool. His tone became a little catty whenever we discussed the local canine population, but otherwise he was always very gracious.

He discovered that life could be very stimulating and, on the other hand, very exhausting. His proverbial catnaps stretched into hours, broken only by the necessity of taking a constitutional stroll or checking up on the latest contents of his dish.

He was clearly annoyed whenever anyone ruffled up his gray velour "tom johns," for he took great pains making himself presentable to society, tending to his various grooming needs with meticulous care.

Once in awhile he humored the young fry by frolicking about like a clumsy kitten, chasing marbles under the bed or pouncing on a toy mouse.

But, mostly, he was just himself, an affectionate old tom-cat who had made a place for himself in the family. No apologies. No regrets.

As friend hubby prepared to take him to the vet, he walked over to the box, jumped in of his own accord, and settled down for the ride. No fears. No fuss.

It was a great way to go.

One could argue that he didn't realize his fate, and one would have a very valid point. We, as intelligent human beings, however, are warned that there is an eternity to face, and yet we strive desperately to avoid the subject. Is it fear of the unknown, or shame because of our past?

Unlike animals who live by instinct alone, God has given us the ability to choose our destiny. In sharp contrast to the person who meets death with no assurance of salvation, "mark the perfect man, and behold the upright: for the end of that man is peace" (Psalm 37:37, KJV).

Moody Press, a ministry of the Moody Bible Institute
is designed for education, evangelization, and edification.
If we may assist you in knowing more about Christ and
the Christian life, please write us without obligation:
Moody Press, c/o MLM, Chicago, Illinois 60610